J   Folk tales & fables
398.2   of the Middle East
Fol   and Africa.

DATE			
FEB 1 3 1996			
OCT 2 8 1997			
MAR - 2 2002			
MAR 1 2 2006			

FOLK·TALES·&·FABLES·OF
THE MIDDLE EAST AND AFRICA

FOLK·TALES·&·FABLES·OF THE MIDDLE EAST AND AFRICA

Robert Ingpen & Barbara Hayes

CHELSEA HOUSE PUBLISHERS
New York • Philadelphia

First published in the United States in 1994
by Chelsea House Publishers

© Copyright David Bateman Ltd & Dragon's World 1994

First Printing
1 3 5 7 9 8 6 4 2

Text Editor Molly Perham
Editor Diana Briscoe
Art Director Dave Allen
Editorial Director Pippa Rubinstein

ISBN 0-7910-2758-9

Typeset in Bookman.
Printed in Italy

Contents

The Middle East

1 Gilgamesh the King 12

2 David and Goliath 25

3 Aladdin and the Wonderful Lamp 32

4 Joseph Who Dreamed the Truth 48

Africa

5 The Battles of Horus 62

6 The Cunning Monkey 68

7 The Story of Untombinde 70

8 The Horns of Plenty 76

9 The Proud Princess 80

10 Tricky Mr Rabbit 86

11 The Cunning Man 90

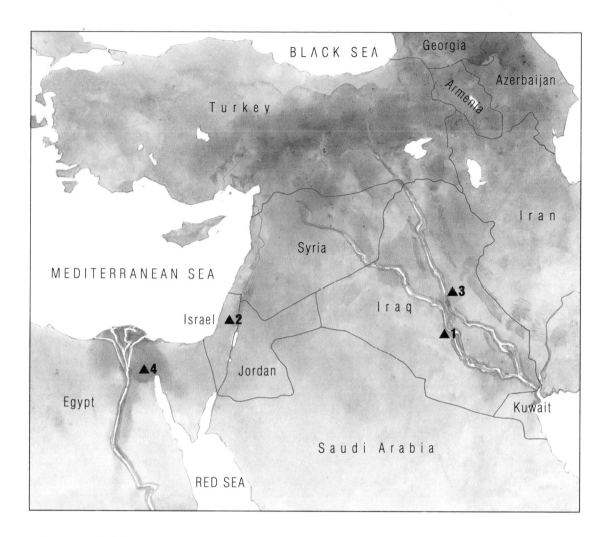

The Middle East

1 Gilgamesh the King
2 David and Goliath
3 Aladdin and the Wonderful Lamp
4 Joseph Who Dreamed the Truth

1

Gilgamesh the King

It is thought that The Epic of Gilgamesh *was first written down about 2100 BC in the library of King Assur-bani-pal in ancient Nineveh, now in Iraq. Undoubtedly, it was told by storytellers long before that. Not long after the twelve clay tablets that recorded the story of Gilgamesh were inscribed, Nineveh fell to invaders. In the tradition of conquering hordes, they burned the library and trampled the clay tablets into the dust under their horses' hooves.*

Buried beneath the debris for nearly 4000 years, the broken tablets lay untouched until they were discovered and pieced together by European excavators in the nineteenth century. Part of the story is missing and we do not understand the ancient Assyrian language completely but the story of Gilgamesh shines through these difficulties.

Gilgamesh was a hero. He rescued the city of Erech from siege by an invading army, then he became its king. He was a brave and clever warrior, but as a ruler he was harsh and unrelenting. Everyone had to obey Gilgamesh's commands or they suffered pain and hardship. To the strong went the spoils, and Gilgamesh was strong. This was the way the people liked things to be, for while Gilgamesh ruled, they need not fear their enemies.

Gilgamesh was the son of the daughter of old King Sokkaros, but no one could say who Gilgamesh's father was. Was it the god of the sun? Was it the eagle that saved the baby's life when he was flung from the top of a high tower? Before Gilgamesh the gods restrained their anger. Strange warriors, whose fierce looks shrivelled other men, stood aside to let Gilgamesh pass. Surely Gilgamesh was related to the shining gods, or why else would his enemies tremble before him?

Like all other mortal men, Sokkaros died and his grandson, Gilgamesh, drove out the enemies who had been harrying the old man in his declining years. Gilgamesh wore precious jewels and gold necklaces, and his clothes were the finest that money could buy. He was a man of the city, and his glory dazzled the people.

However, there were some who forgot how recently the enemy

had been at the gate. They begged the goddess Aruru to send another hero – a man who would defy Gilgamesh, and frighten him into changing his harsh ways.

At last, tired of the constant whining and pleading, Aruru gave their request some thought. Inside her head she created a picture of a man totally unlike Gilgamesh. Then she washed her hands, took some clay, and shaped it in the likeness of that man. She threw the clay to the ground in a far mountain country. That was how Enkidu, the wild man, was created.

Enkidu lived just like an animal. He hunted for his food in the scrubland, eating plants alongside the herds of gazelles, and drinking at waterholes with the animals of the desert. His body was hairy all over, and the hair on his head reached to his waist like that of a woman. But, he wore the clothes of a god, for the goddess Aruru had created him.

Enkidu lived in the wilderness away from the protected life of the city and he grew strong and fierce. Tales of the wild man who ran faster than the animals and swam swifter than the silver fish reached Gilgamesh. Perhaps his father, Shamash, god of the sun, had warned him that Enkidu had been sent to humble him. Gilgamesh became suspicious, so he sent a skilled tracker, called Tsaidu, and a beautiful girl from the temple of the goddess Ishtar, Ukhut, to find Enkidu.

'Tempt him with stories of life in the city,' said Gilgamesh. 'Get him into your power, then bring him to Erech so that I may look at this rival.'

Tsaidu and the beautiful Ukhut travelled into the wilderness. They waited at the watering hole where Enkidu usually drank, and saw him lean down and lap water like the beasts. They walked in front of him in their graceful silks and lovely jewels. Ukhut's soft hair was shining and smooth, not stiff and rough like the hair of the creatures in the wilderness. Her skin, sheltered by the walls that surrounded the temple of Ishtar, was delicate, not coarse from the sun.

Enkidu fell in love with Ukhut. For six days and seven nights he stayed with her at the waterhole, listening to stories of life in the city. He longed to visit this place where men lived.

'Come with us to stay in the city and visit the great Gilgamesh,' urged Ukhut and Tsaidu.

Suddenly Enkidu remembered his friends – the gazelles, the water beasts and the herds of animals – and ran to speak to them. Some had moved on, while most of the rest had forgotten him in the short time he had spent with Ukhut. Those who did remember him would no longer obey him.

'Where were you for six days and seven nights?' they asked. 'One who comes and goes is no use to us.'

Ukhut and Tsaidu said again, 'Come with us. You are very handsome. Why waste your good looks on the beasts? Come to the great palace and meet Gilgamesh, that dazzling ruler of men.'

So Enkidu agreed to go to the town. On the way the gods whispered in his ear. 'You were created to humble Gilgamesh,' they said. 'Be prepared to fight him.'

Enkidu had a mind of his own. Life in the city sounded alluring and he wanted Gilgamesh to be his friend. Enkidu thought of the customs of the animals, the only customs he knew. When two strong animals met, they always fought before they could be friends. A combat would settle which of them was to be the leader. Perhaps I should challenge Gilgamesh to a duel so that we will know from the start which of us is the greater, thought Enkidu.

He asked the opinion of Ukhut, who knew about the ways of the city. 'Fight Gilgamesh, if you must,' she said, 'but remember he is strong and aggressive. He has an army of guards lining the walls of his palace. He is not a man to take orders from others, and most important of all, he is loved by the god, Shamash.'

Enkidu didn't mention fighting Gilgamesh again – he was a wise young man.

Meanwhile, Gilgamesh eagerly waited for the arrival of the

hairy man of the wilderness, whom the goddess Aruru had created especially to humble him. Should he kill him, or imprison him, or surround him with so much luxury that he would become a weakling? It was not an easy decision. He had to take care not to offend Aruru.

Even the plans of a powerful goddess may go awry. When Gilgamesh and Enkidu met, they found they liked each other. Gilgamesh gave up his plans to harm Enkidu and Enkidu never thought of humbling Gilgamesh. They loved each other like brothers from the first meeting.

Once, as was only natural, Enkidu became homesick for the freedom of the open country. When he spoke of leaving the city, the sun god, Shamash, intervened. He appeared as a vision to the two young men. 'Enkidu will stay in comfort in the palace,' he said. 'Gilgamesh will give him a seat next to the throne and the kings who come to pay tribute will kiss Enkidu's feet.'

So it was done and Enkidu stayed in the city of Erech.

Then Enkidu started to have a recurring dream. In his dream he saw a frightful monster pawing at the foot of the sacred cedar tree that guarded the forest home of the goddess Ishtar. At the same time Shamash whispered into Gilgamesh's ear, 'Do not rest here. Go to the forest and slay the monster, Humbaba.' Both young men knew that they had been set a terrible task.

Gilgamesh knew that the gods have devious ways, so he went to consult his mother, the priestess Rimat-belit. He asked her advice on how to reach the Forest of Cedars, and which path to take to the sacred tree and the home of Ishtar. Rimat-belit, who had kept company with the gods in her youth, told her dear son all that she knew. She watched him leave, and her heart went with him.

Then she turned and called out to Shamash, 'Why did you choose my son for this terrible task?' she asked. 'Couldn't you find someone else to risk his life? You have sent my dearest boy to fight that frightful monster. Now you must watch over him every moment he is away. Don't turn your attention to other things. Use all your superhuman powers to care for our son until he returns to his home.'

Gilgamesh and Enkidu found their way to the Forest of Cedars. It was a still, silent place, for Humbata's invisible power had spread through the trees like an ill wind. Anyone who entered the forest felt weak and sick long before they saw the

monster. After walking for only a short while, Enkidu collapsed at the wayside. 'I am ill,' he said. 'My arms are weak. My hands will not do what I tell them.'

No harm came to Gilgamesh because the god Shamash had heard Rimat-belit's prayers and was watching over him. Gilgamesh strode through the forest, unharmed, found the frightful monster and slew it. Enkidu struggled forward to be with his friend, but he was weak and helpless.

Gilgamesh returned in triumph to the city of Erech. He walked every step of the way wearing the blood-stained, torn clothes in which he had fought the monster, and his friend Enkidu trailed like a shadow behind him.

Gilgamesh walked through the streets of Erech showing off his gory apparel and boasting of his valiant deed. Then he took off the torn clothes and washed away the blood. He put on his golden kingly robes and wore flowers of victory round his brow. He had never looked more noble or more handsome – and in that moment the seeds of his future sorrows were sown.

The goddess Ishtar looked down to see the hero who had slain the terrible monster at her door. When she saw how handsome Gilgamesh was, she fell in love with him. She came to the palace and asked Gilgamesh to be her husband. 'I am a goddess,' she said. 'Marry me and your flocks will increase, your enemies will flee and all nations will pay tribute to you.'

Gilgamesh laughed. 'That may be so,' he said, 'but for how long? You have had many husbands, and you have tired of all of them. You have cast them aside and taken their riches for your own. Why should my fate be different? I will not marry you.'

Ishtar returned to heaven in a rage at being scorned. She whispered spiteful words into the ears of the other gods and turned many of them against Gilgamesh.

'Gilgamesh must be punished for his impudence,' said Anu, the King of the Gods. At Ishtar's request, he created a mighty bull, the Bull of Heaven, whose breath would spoil the crops of the earth for seven years, and sent the bull to fight Gilgamesh.

'Kill the bull,' he said to Gilgamesh. 'If you do not, he will kill you. Then he will rampage through your lands and they will lie fallow for seven years.'

Gilgamesh was a hero. He felt not one moment of doubt and, taking up his weapons, went to face the bull. The fight was long and exhausting. Dirt kicked up by the bull choked Gilgamesh's throat, sweat ran down his forehead and blurred his eyes, and blood ran from his wounds. But Gilgamesh killed that huge bull before the bull could kill him.

Enkidu, who was still sick, could only stand and watch.

The scorned goddess Ishtar burned with fury. She stood on the walls of Erech and screeched at Gilgamesh, 'Curse you! Curse you, who have scorned me! How dare you be strong enough to defeat a bull sent by the gods! You will be punished!'

At that Enkidu found the strength to defy Ishtar. 'Gilgamesh defeated the bull in a fair fight,' he said. 'That should be the end of the matter. You are wrong to carry on with the feud. Leave Gilgamesh in peace.'

Ishtar turned flaming red with fury and her hair rose like a lion's mane about her head. 'Curse you too!' she hissed at Enkidu. From that moment there was no more hope for his life.

The beautiful Ukhut, who had seduced Enkidu beside the waterhole, was already dead. She came to Enkidu one night in a dream. 'Enkidu,' she said, 'it is time for you to come with me down to the land of the shadows. Come with me down the path of no return, to the house where no one who enters ever leaves. Now you must live in the land without light, where dust is our food and the feathers of the birds are our clothes.'

Enkidu did not rise from his bed again. Twelve days later, he was dead.

Gilgamesh was grief stricken. He would never walk in the sunlight with his dear friend again. No one was left with whom he shared the same memories because part of his own life was lying in the grave with Enkidu.

Suddenly Gilgamesh was seized with a great fear of death. He decided to seek out his ancestor, Ut-Napishtim, the only man ever to be made immortal by the gods. Ut-Napishtim must tell me the secret of everlasting life, thought Gilgamesh. Death must not take me to the land of shadows.

Finding the home of an immortal is not easy. Immortals never die – they do not live or eat or drink as other men do. And they guard their secrets carefully. Gilgamesh walked towards the lonely, forbidden place. The land rose from the plain into high mountains, and the rocky slopes of the valleys pressed menacingly on either side. Wild beasts grunted and stalked what looked like an easy meal. This was the country Enkidu had loved. The wild man would have known every trick used by the wild animals, but Enkidu was no longer with Gilgamesh.

Sin, the moon god, slipped down from the sky and, taking Gilgamesh by the hand, led him through that place of peril. When they came to Mashu, the Mountain of the Sunset, even the moon god would not stay. 'Go no further, Gilgamesh,' he said. 'This is a place of danger.'

Gilgamesh would not turn back. He looked towards the sky that was spread with the fires of sunset. By day and by night the pink and mauve clouds hung above Mount Mashu. No one could explain why, but they were always there. This was the entrance to the far world where life was different, where men were not as other men, and where the immortals lived.

Gilgamesh stepped forward and his path was barred by the Scorpion men. These terrifying creatures had a human shape, but were covered with shimmering, shining skin like that of a scorpion. They shrivelled men up with their gaze and to look on them was death. They guarded the slopes of Mount Mashu from

sunrise to sunset, as they were the servants of the sun. There were so many that they covered the mountainside.

Gilgamesh looked at them and was afraid. They dazzled him and he became confused, but he did not die under their gaze because he was partly a god. Seeing that this was no ordinary man, the Scorpion men came forward and spoke to Gilgamesh. He told them that he was seeking his ancestor, Ut-Napishtim, in order to learn the secrets of immortality.

'Go back,' counselled the Scorpion men. 'Ut-Napishtim does live beyond the slopes of Mashu, beyond the land of the sunset, but you will never survive the journey. After the sunset you will come to a land of darkness. For twenty-four hours you will travel through the night – a terrible choking night – and more barriers lie beyond that. If we let you through, we will be sending you to your death.'

Gilgamesh stumbled to his feet. 'I am going forward,' he said. His manner was rough and his eyes were threatening. Even in his grief and confusion, Gilgamesh was still the man who had ruled Erech with a hand of iron. The Scorpion men stood aside and let him walk through.

Gilgamesh walked under the flaming sunset and into the thick, choking darkness of the land of night. On and on he went and at last the blackness lightened. A faint gleam, then a strong light, filled the sky and Gilgamesh found himself in a beautiful garden. It was lovely, but it was strange because nothing was real. The leaves on the trees were made from lapis lazuli and the fruit was made of rubies and sapphires. These are the gardens of the gods, thought Gilgamesh.

Gilgamesh was tired and dirty; his clothes were torn and his legs were bleeding from his many falls in the darkness. He still grieved for his dead friend, Enkidu, and he was anxious to find the right road to the home of his ancestor, Ut-Napishtim.

Siduri, the goddess of the sea, looked out from her palace on the seashore and saw the unhappy figure of Gilgamesh. She saw a desperate man torn by deep emotions, yet still ferocious and menacing. Siduri locked her doors and pulled down the shutters over the windows. This trouble I can do without, she thought.

Gilgamesh reached the shore and looked at the ocean before him. His father, Shamash, whispered in his ear, 'You must cross the sea to reach Ut-Napishtim. To do that you need the advice of Siduri, the goddess of the sea.'

Gilgamesh walked to the sea-bleached doors of the palace. He knocked. He called. He hammered and shouted. Still Siduri would not let him in. A man who can get this far into our different world is a man to be feared, she thought.

She was right. The same fury that had made Gilgamesh the conqueror of Erech consumed him now. He raised his axe and brought it down with a crash, splintering the palace doors. 'Let me in or I will destroy your precious home,' he shouted.

At once Siduri ordered the doors to be opened and food was set before Gilgamesh. Trembling with fright, she asked him what he wanted.

'Tell me how to cross the water to reach my ancestor, the immortal Ut-Napishtim,' he replied.

'Do not go,' said Siduri. 'It is too dangerous. Already you have come too far into this strange land. You do not know the peril you are in. Return to your home while you still have the strength.'

Gilgamesh would not listen.

'Very well then,' said Siduri, 'Adad-Ea is the ferryman of Ut-Napishtim. He is the only one who can take you across these treacherous waters. Ask him to ferry you to the far shore.'

Adad-Ea was as reluctant as Siduri to help this desperate man who had come out of the great darkness. 'Go home and do not bother me,' he said.

Gilgamesh raised his axe and smashed the rudder from Adad-Ea's boat. Then he turned and looked at the ferryman. 'Take me across to Ut-Napishtim or I will smash the rest of your boat and you will never take anyone anywhere again,' he said.

Adad-Ea hastily agreed. Gilgamesh cut him a new rudder from the forest and they sailed across the water.

Ut-Napishtim was surprised to see the boat approaching because it was not the time for Adad-Ea to visit. He was even more amazed when he saw Gilgamesh in the boat.

Eagerly Gilgamesh rose to his feet, planning to wade ashore to talk to this man who knew the secret of immortality, but he was too weak to scramble over the side of the boat. He felt sick.

Seasick!' he groaned. 'I must be seasick. How strange! I have never been seasick before.'

Adad-Ea looked at his unwanted

passenger. 'It is not seasickness that ails you,' he said. 'Look at your skin.' Gilgamesh looked down and found that he was covered in sores.

'You should never have come,' said Adad-Ea. 'Everyone told you that, from the Scorpion men onwards, but you knew better.'

Gilgamesh gripped the side of the boat and pulled himself up so that he could talk to his ancestor. I have come so far and suffered so much, and I will find out the secret, he thought.

'Greetings, noble ancestor,' he called, 'I am Gilgamesh, a great warrior and worthy descendant of your noble self. The gods granted immortality to you. Tell me why, so that I too may earn this precious gift.'

Ut-Napishtim shifted from foot to foot. 'You look unwell,' he said. 'This is not the time to talk. Sleep for a while. We will discuss your question later.'

Gilgamesh would not be deterred. 'Tell me the secret of immortality!' he shouted.

'Be reasonable!' begged Ut-Napishtim. 'How can I do such a thing? The gods would be furious. Death is the destiny of all mankind. Man cannot avoid death, or know when it will strike. The gods decide these things. It is not for you or me to interfere. Take my word for it, immortality is not so desirable a thing.'

Gilgamesh broke into a cold sweat and the sickness made his head ache. The sores on his body stung, but still he clung to the side of the boat and shouted across the shallow water, 'Undesirable or not, I notice you did not refuse immortality when it was offered to you. Why is it good for you, but not for me?'

'I was very special,' protested Ut-Napishtim. 'I was picked out by the god Ea. He ordered me to build a big ship and take people and animals into it. I did as I was told and when a great flood covered the earth, everyone on my boat lived. If it had not been for me, all animals and humans would have perished. The gods made me and my wife immortal in thanks. I cannot ask them to do it for you. You may be a great warrior, but so are other men.'

Gilgamesh was disappointed. For once his ferocious spirit flagged and his head drooped. Ut-Napishtim felt sorry for him. 'Come ashore and I will try to heal you,' he said.

Gilgamesh was carried to a bed. Ut-Napishtim ordered sleep to breathe upon him. For six days and nights Gilgamesh slept, while Ut-Napishtim's wife treated his sores with ointment.

When Gilgamesh woke up, he was taken to a special spring where he bathed. His sores were finally healed and his strength restored. Once more he asked for the secret of immortality. 'The gods will not grant it to you,' replied Ut-Napishtim. 'It is useless to ask.'

Ut-Napishtim's wife smiled at Gilgamesh's handsome face. 'There is a plant growing at the bottom of the sea,' she whispered, 'Adad-Ea knows where to find it. Eat this plant and you will never grow old.' With this Gilgamesh had to be satisfied.

Adad-Ea showed him how to collect the prickly sea-plant from the bottom of the ocean. They made a great bundle of it and then Adad-Ea guided Gilgamesh back to the land of men.

As he came within sight of Erech, Gilgamesh found a spring of sweet water. He knelt and put the precious bundle down beside him. Then he gave thanks to the gods for bringing him safely home from such a perilous journey. As Gilgamesh prayed, a serpent scented the sea-plant and, slithering forward, carried the bundle away in its mouth. Gilgamesh never saw the magic herb again. He wept bitterly because it was clear that the gods did not intend him to be immortal.

Gilgamesh strode into Erech. Everywhere he looked he was reminded of Enkidu and his grief returned. He went from temple to temple begging the gods to let Enkidu come back to him. At last Ea, the god of wisdom, agreed. A hole opened up in a hillside, a cold wind blew and suddenly Enkidu was standing in the sunlight – a pale grey shadow of the living Enkidu.

'Do not waste your time in grief,' he said to Gilgamesh. 'I am a fortunate spirit. You gave me proper burial and put furnishings and clothes and food in my tomb. In the land of shadows I live in luxury with delicious meals to eat and fine clothes to wear. You saved me from the shame of those whose bodies are left to rot in the fields. They are beggars in the other world and have no comforts.' Enkidu smiled, turned away and then was gone.

So ends the story of Gilgamesh. Hopefully he found happiness during the rest of his life. Or did he spend his time gazing at the eternal sunset over Mount Mashu, longing for immortality?

2
David and Goliath

The story of David and Goliath is one of the most vivid in the Old Testament. There are many other stories about David. They tell how he became King and had children, including Solomon who built the first temple in Jerusalem. King David also wrote many of the beautiful poems that are preserved in the Book of Psalms.

Long, long ago, Samuel was a prophet who gave God's messages to the Jewish people and Saul was their King. However, Saul sinned and God turned away from him. Then the Lord told Samuel to go to Bethlehem to anoint a new King, whom he would find among the sons of a man named Jesse.

Samuel went to Bethlehem and, seeking out Jesse, asked him to bring his sons to join him in making a sacrifice to the Lord. Out of respect for the prophet, Jesse did as he was asked. One by one Samuel looked at Jesse's sons, but as each one passed before him, Samuel heard the Lord whispering in his ear, 'Do not be deceived by this man's handsome face, nor his fine build. You see his outside appearance, but God looks into men's hearts.'

Seven sons of Jesse walked before Samuel, but none of them pleased the Lord.

'Have you no other sons?' Samuel asked Jesse.

'I do have one other,' replied Jesse, 'but he is only a lad and he is out tending the sheep.'

'Then bring him to me,' said Samuel. 'I must see all your sons, even the youngest.'

He waited impatiently until the boy came and stood before him. The boy's face was glowing with good health and his glossy hair hung down on either side of his beautiful face.

'Anoint this boy,' said the Lord. 'He is the one.'

Meanwhile King Saul, unaware of the prophet's task, was becoming more and more troubled. His mind was disturbed and he suffered from fits of rage. He terrified everybody around him.

'Music will help me,' said Saul. 'If only someone would find a man who could play sweet music. I am surrounded by fools. When they drive me to madness I need music – soft, peaceful music – to calm my shattered nerves.'

One of his servants found the courage to speak. 'It is said that David, the son of Jesse of Bethlehem, plays music that charms the ear,' he whispered. 'He is also brave, clever and handsome and is loved by the Lord.'

'Yes, yes,' snapped Saul, who was used to hearing people's virtues exaggerated. 'If he can play sweet music, send for him.'

Messengers left the King's court and fetched the boy David from where he was still tending his father's sheep. He stood before King Saul and the King was pleased with what he saw.

'You will be my armour-bearer,' said King Saul, 'and you will stay by my side. You will keep this harp close to hand and when the fits of madness come upon me, you will play. Sooth the demons in my head with sweet music and make me well again.'

So David stayed at the court of King Saul.

In those far off days there were frequent battles. Before David had been at court for very long, the Philistines gathered a large army together and marched on the land of the Jews. King Saul summoned his soldiers and went to face his enemies. Each army stood in formation on a mountain slope, with a valley between them. Then both sides hesitated, for neither of them wanted to strike the first blow.

Then a champion strode out from the Philistin' camp. He was a giant of a man called Goliath of Gath. He was a magnificent and terrifying sight. He wore a brass helmet on his head and a coat of mail that would have weighed any other man to the ground. Brass armour protected his shins and his breast, and he brandished a spear like a battering ram. His shield-bearer walked in front of him with confident insolence. Goliath ran his eyes over King Saul's army. To and fro he looked, taking his time.

At last he called in his booming voice, 'Why are you bothering to stand in battle array, you midgets of King Saul? There is no need for you to try and fight. Here am I, a champion of the Philistines, ready and willing. Send out a champion of your own against me. Then none of the rest of you mice need raise a sword. If your warrior kills me, then we will be your servants. If I kill him, you will be our servants. In this way the blood of only one man need be shed. I lay this challenge before Saul's army. Send one champion against me and let us settle the quarrel.'

His voice died away into a long, long silence. Neither King Saul nor any of his men stepped forward. With good reason, they were all afraid of Goliath of Gath.

Now David, the son of Jesse of Bethlehem, was still a boy and not old enough to march with the army. Finding himself left behind and not needed by King Saul, he took the opportunity to visit his father. He was very welcome, for his three eldest brothers had gone to fight the Philistines.

'We are short of hands to help with the sheep,' said Jesse. 'Go out and tend them, David.'

Forty days went by, but still the three older boys had not returned, nor was there any news of their fate. The truth was that the armies had reached stalemate. Each stood in formation on the mountainside and each day Goliath of Gath paraded up and down the valley calling for a champion to come down and fight. No one dared to accept his invitation.

In those days, when men turned out to defend their country, they took their own food along with them. Whatever the outcome, good or bad, the campaigns were at least short. After forty days, Jesse became concerned that his three sons were running out of food. He gave David a supply of loaves and cheeses and told him to find the army and give the food to his brothers.

On the day that David found the army, the men were preparing to do battle. No one was willing to fight Goliath alone and the only alternative was a full pitched battle. David hurried from group to group, asking for his brothers. He heard the talk about Goliath and how no one dared fight him, not even King Saul himself. Now the whole army was going to have to fight.

He looked into the valley and saw a huge man swaggering up and down with his shield-bearer walking in front of him. Is that Goliath? wondered David, thinking that he looked too pleased

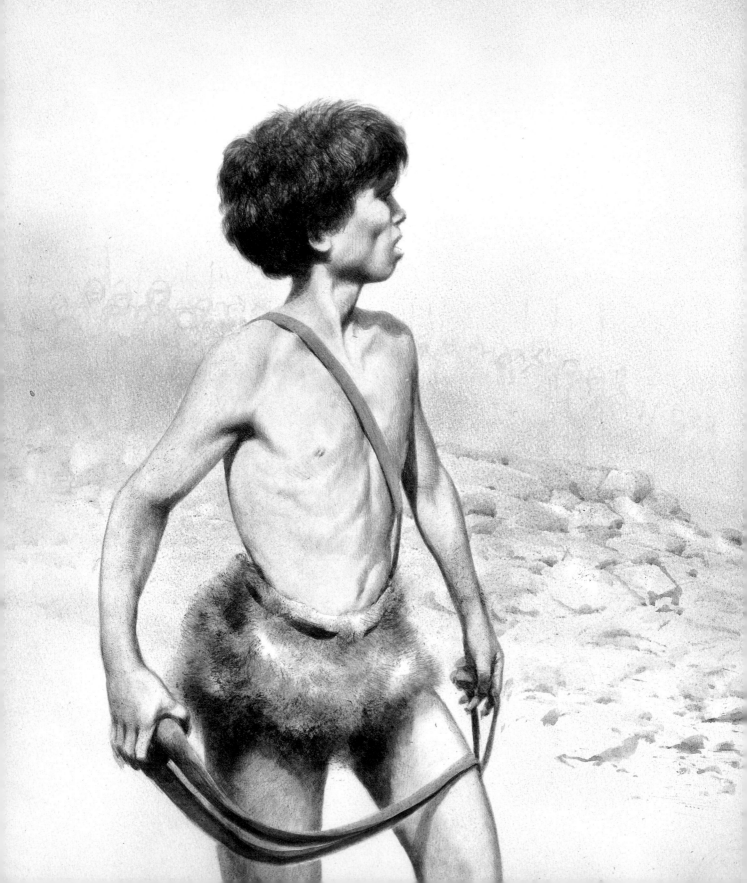

with himself to be a real hero. David hurried along the hillside, searching for his brothers. He kept glancing down at Goliath.

'Do you mean to say everyone in the army is frightened of that man?' he asked. From the descriptions of Goliath, he had expected to see a monster breathing fire, rather than a flesh and blood man.

Goliath's thundering voice jeered and laughed at King Saul's army, and David burned with fury.

'What is the reward for the man who goes down and silences that man who is mocking our nation?' he asked.

A group of soldiers laughed at David. 'Whoever kills Goliath will be loaded with riches and marry a daughter of King Saul,' they said. 'But you look a little young for the job.'

At last David found his eldest brother, Eliab. Eliab was astounded to see the boy in such a dangerous place.

'What are you doing here?' he gasped. 'You should be back with the sheep. Oh, I know. You have slipped away to watch the fun. Well, fighting is a man's work. Go home and keep out of this.'

David was annoyed at such a reception. 'Fine words to greet me when I have come all this way to bring you food,' he said. 'And as for this being no place for me, well I disagree. If no-one else is willing to fight Goliath, then it is fortunate that I have arrived.'

He went and stood before King Saul. 'There is no need for anyone to fear Goliath,' he said. 'I, your majesty's servant, will fight that boasting Philistine.'

King Saul shook his head. 'You are only a boy,' he said. 'You cannot fight a trained soldier.'

David stood his ground. 'A shepherd boy I may be,' he said, 'but shepherd boys know how to fight. Lions and bears come to take my father's sheep, but I kill them first. If I can kill a lion and a bear, why should I not kill this impudent Philistine who dares to challenge the Lord's chosen people?'

King Saul sat in silence. 'Go out to fight,' he said at last, 'and may God be with you.'

The King gave David his own helmet and coat of mail, thinking to help the young boy. David put them on, but took no more than two steps. 'These are no good for me,' he said. 'They weigh me down and make me feel awkward.'

He took off the armour and stood in his shepherd clothes. He swung his sling in one hand and a stick in the other. He put five smooth stones in a pouch at his side. He smiled at King Saul and the soldiers. 'I will go like this,' he said. 'It is better.'

The young boy walked down the hill into the valley to confront Goliath, the great warrior of Gath. Goliath was surprised to see a lad walking towards him and did not at first realise that this was a champion from Saul's army.

'Go home, boy,' he laughed.

When he understood that David did indeed intend to challenge him, he was furious. 'Am I a dog,' he roared, 'that a shepherd with a stick is sent to drive me off? Come here, boy, and let me tear you apart and throw your limbs to the birds of the air and the beasts of the fields.'

David felt no fear. 'You come armed with sword and spear and have a shield to protect you,' he called in his clear, young voice, 'but I come against you with the Lord of Hosts at my side. God will deliver you into my hands.'

Then Goliath said no more, but set his mouth in a straight line. The time for talking was over. Boy or not, this challenger who talked so big must be cut to pieces. Goliath walked forward, a trained soldier eager to do his work.

David walked towards Goliath. He was not trained so he did not know the rules. He did not take up a battle stance but looked at Goliath with the eyes of a shepherd boy looking at a lion. He did not know the correct way to parry a sword, or how to deflect a spear, but he did see that Goliath's forehead was not protected by armour.

Taking a stone from his pouch, David put it in his sling and aimed at Goliath's face. The stone knocked him unconscious. The great man pitched to the ground and fell on his face. David ran to him and, snatching up his sword, hacked Goliath's head from his shoulders. The fight was over almost before the watchers knew that it had started.

The Philistine army turned and fled in fear and the land of Israel was saved from invasion. David was made a captain in Saul's army. A glittering future lay ahead of him. But King Saul was jealous, for David had been victorious, while he had been shamed. David's future was not to be an easy one.

3

Aladdin and the Wonderful Lamp

The stories of The Arabian Nights *are supposed to have been told by the Sultana Scheherazade over 1001 nights. She did this to intrigue her husband, the Sultan of Baghdad, so that he would not have her executed. The Sultan had killed his many previous wives to prevent them from being unfaithful to him. There was an Arab community in China, mostly living in and around Canton, from the thirteenth century onwards. They traded in silks and other rich fabrics and in spices.*

A poor tailor called Mustapha lived in China a long time ago. He worked hard and made a modest living for his wife and only child. However, his son, Aladdin, was a wild and wayward boy, who preferred to spend his days playing in the streets and chatting to his friends in the public square, rather than working in his father's tailor's shop.

Then, worn out with work and worry, Mustapha died. Now there was nobody to restrain Aladdin, because he took no notice of his gentle mother. The boy made no attempt to work or learn a trade, but ran wild in the streets with a gang of idle youths. His poor mother earned what money she could, but their home became threadbare and often there was no food in the cupboard.

When Aladdin was fifteen years old, a stranger came to town. He was a sorcerer from Africa. This man watched the youths who ran wild in the streets and saw something in Aladdin's face that suited his purpose. He talked to the merchants in the market place and learned much of Aladdin's family history.

Then, wearing his finest clothes and his richest jewels, the sorcerer approached Aladdin and asked, 'My dear boy, is your name Aladdin and are you the son of Mustapha, the tailor?'

Impressed by the apparent wealth of the stranger, Aladdin replied that this was so, but that his father was now dead.

At once the sorcerer threw his arms round the boy's neck and with tears in his eyes cried, 'Then you are my nephew. Your father, Mustapha, was my dear brother. Oh, how grieved I am that he is dead and that I shall never see him again!'

The sorcerer asked Aladdin where he lived, gave him some money for his mother and said that he would have supper with them the next evening. Aladdin ran home and told his mother about the rich and generous uncle who was coming to visit them.

His mother was puzzled and suspicious. 'Your father had no brother, nor did I,' she said. 'You have no uncles. This man has made a mistake.' However, she could not resist taking the money. She bought food and made a good supper for the next evening.

At suppertime the sorcerer arrived with gifts of fruit and wine, and more gold coins that he gave to Aladdin. He gave presents of jewels to Aladdin's mother and assured her that he really was Mustapha's brother, and that he had been out of the country for thirty years travelling in Africa and India.

The poor woman could think of no reason why this rich stranger should help them unless his story were true. She took the gifts and hoped that their days of poverty were over. The three of them ate supper together and then the sorcerer left, promising to visit again the next day.

So things continued for several days, until Aladdin and his mother trusted the so-called uncle completely. Then the cunning sorcerer started to put his plan into effect.

'Aladdin,' he said one bright morning. 'This humble home in which you and your mother live is not good enough. Come with me and we will choose a fine mansion with lovely gardens where the three of us may live together with servants to wait on us. You

are all the family I have left and I want to take care of you.'

This sounded very agreeable to Aladdin and, putting on some of the fine clothes the sorcerer had bought for him, he said goodbye to his mother and walked out through the city gates. On and on they walked, and although Aladdin saw many houses that seemed suitable to him, his uncle found fault with all of them and led the boy further and further from the city.

At last they reached the foothills of the mountains and, as the sorcerer had intended from the beginning, they stopped in a narrow valley between two low hills. This was the place that the sorcerer had seen in his dreams. He had travelled all the way from Africa to find it.

Turning to Aladdin, he said, 'Gather some dry sticks and make a fire. I am going to show you many wonderful and frightening things, but you will thank me in the end.'

Aladdin was puzzled, but did as his uncle said and soon a great fire was blazing. The sorcerer threw some incense on the flames and chanted magic words. At once the earth before him rolled back to reveal a stone with a ring fixed in the centre. Terrified, Aladdin turned to run, but his uncle caught him by the arm and gave him a blow round the ears and told him to stay close. This seemed a strange way for a man to behave who, until then, had been so kind.

'Remember, I am your uncle and you should obey me as if I were your father,' snarled the sorcerer. Then he went on on in a more wheedling tone, 'Aladdin, under this stone there is a great treasure and only you may enter to get it. Do not be afraid. If you do exactly as I say, no harm will come to you, only great riches.'

The talk of treasure calmed Aladdin's fears and he agreed to do as his uncle instructed. The sorcerer pointed at the stone. 'Take hold of the ring and lift the stone,' he said.

Aladdin could not help laughing. 'Uncle!' he gasped. 'How can I lift such a heavy weight? You must help me.'

'No!' snapped the sorcerer, again letting his mask of kindness slip. 'You must do it alone. If I help you, everything will be ruined. Pull on the ring and the stone will rise. Try it and see.'

Lured by the thought of riches, Aladdin pulled on the ring. To his amazement the stone swung back easily to reveal a short staircase leading down to a door.

'Go down the stairs and open the door,' said the sorcerer. 'Go through and you will find yourself in a palace with three great halls. On either side of you there will be gold and silver, but you must not touch it. Walk carefully through the halls. Take nothing, and do not let your clothes brush against anything. You will then enter a garden. In the garden will be many lovely fruit trees, but you must walk to the far side where you will find a lamp burning in a niche. Blow out the lamp and throw away the wick and the oil. Put the lamp in your waistband and hurry back here.'

As Aladdin started to go down the steps, the sorcerer called him back. He pulled off a ring and placed it on one of Aladdin's fingers. 'This is a magic ring,' he said. 'It will keep you safe from danger. Now hurry through the palace and bring back the lamp and we will both become rich.'

Aladdin descended the steps and pushed open the door. He found himself in a magnificent palace, exactly as his uncle had described. On either side were jars containing silver and gold coins, but the boy touched none of them. Gathering his clothes closely about him, Aladdin hastened through the three halls and out into the garden.

Still doing exactly what his uncle had told him, the boy walked across the garden to the place where a lamp burned in a niche. He took the lamp, blew out the light, threw away the wick and the oil, then tucked the lamp into his waistband. However Aladdin could not help staring at the fruits hanging from the trees. Some were milky white, some hung in green clusters, some glittered like crystal, and some were as red as strawberries. My uncle did not forbid me to touch the fruit in the garden, thought Aladdin. I will take some home to my mother.

He wandered among the trees picking handfuls of the pretty fruit. He was disappointed to find that they were hard and not like the soft, luscious fruit he had expected, but he took them anyway. Aladdin did not know that the milky white fruits were pearls, the green fruits were emeralds, the crystal fruits were diamonds and the red berries were rubies.

Aladdin filled his waistband and the front of his jacket with as many fruits as he could fit in, then hurried back to where the

sorcerer waited. At the foot of the steep flight of steps, Aladdin paused for breath.

'Give me your hand and help me up Uncle,' he panted.

'Give me the lamp first,' snapped the sorcerer, whose temper was frayed from waiting.

The lamp was buried under the fruits Aladdin had picked in the garden. 'Oh, I cannot get it out now,' he called. 'I will give it to you as soon as I am out of this hole.'

At this the sorcerer lost his temper completely and, convinced that Aladdin was trying to cheat him of the lamp, he threw more incense on the fire and chanted some magic words. At once the

stone closed over the staircase and the earth rolled back over the stone as if it had never been disturbed. Aladdin was trapped.

'Let the little wretch rot underground,' fumed the furious sorcerer, as he hurried away. Still shaking with rage, he went back to Africa, carefully avoiding Aladdin's home town in case anyone should enquire after the boy.

The truth was that the sorcerer had learned about the lamp from studying his magic books. He could only gain the lamp if it were given to him willingly by someone who did not know its value. He had chosen Aladdin because of his bold manner. Then, just as it seemed he would gain the prize, Aladdin had refused to give him the lamp and all the sorcerer's hopes were ruined.

Meanwhile, Aladdin was trapped in the darkness below the stone. 'Uncle! Uncle!' he called. 'I will give you the lamp. Let me out.' But there was no one to hear his cries and soon the boy realised that he must help himself. Feeling his way downwards, he tried to push open the door leading to the palace. At least in the palace it is light, he thought, and I might find a way out through the garden. But the door to the palace was shut fast and no banging or pushing would open it.

Poor Aladdin crouched on the steps in the darkness and clasped his hands together, intending to pray to Allah for help. However, in doing so, he rubbed the ring that the sorcerer had given him. Immediately a huge genie appeared and said, 'What is your wish, O Master? I serve whoever wears that ring.'

Frightening though the genie was, Aladdin was delighted to see anyone who might help him escape from the underground darkness. 'Whoever you are, get me out of this place,' he said.

Before he knew what was happening, Aladdin found himself back at the place where he had lit the fire. There was no sign of the opening in the ground, or his cruel uncle. Aladdin hurried home to his mother and at once fell into an exhausted sleep.

The next day when he woke, he told his mother about his adventure and then asked for something to eat. 'I am sorry, son,' she replied, 'there is no food in the house. Now your so-called uncle is gone, there is no one to give us money to buy more.'

Aladdin rummaged among the things he had brought back from the underground palace and picked up the lamp. 'I will take this to sell in the market,' he said. 'It will fetch enough to buy food for a meal or two.'

His mother picked up a cloth. 'Let me polish it for you,' she said. 'It will fetch a better price if it looks shiny and new.'

She had hardly given the lamp one good rub when another genie, even larger than the genie of the ring, stood before them. The huge creature stared down at them. 'I am the slave of the lamp,' it boomed. 'Your wish is my command.'

This was too much for Aladdin's mother and she fainted. Aladdin snatched up the lamp and, holding it in his hands, stared boldly back at the genie. 'I am hungry,' he said. 'Bring me a fine meal.'

The genie disappeared and was back in a few seconds holding a silver tray. On the tray were silver dishes containing delicious food, silver flasks holding good wine and some beautiful silver goblets. The genie set down the tray and vanished.

Aladdin and his mother, when she regained her senses, sat down and enjoyed the meal. Then they talked about what they should do. It was clear that they could become immensely rich with the help of the slave of the lamp. However, they were afraid that they would be accused of stealing. They decided it would be better to live in modest comfort by selling the silver tray and the dishes. They would rub the lamp and ask for more food and silver dishes only when they needed them.

Several years passed and Aladdin grew up a handsome young man. From his visits to the silver merchants he became familiar with fine jewels and he realised that the fruits he had picked in the underground garden were precious gems. He said nothing, but kept them hidden and went on with his contented life.

This might have continued had it not been for Princess Buddir, the only child of the Emperor of China. One day, when Aladdin was out walking, he heard whips cracking and saw the Emperor's servants running along the pavements calling to the shopkeepers to close their shops and shutter their windows.

'Everyone must get off the streets,' shouted the servants. 'Princess Buddir will pass this way to the public baths. No one may look on her face.'

With their whips, they drove all the people indoors – all except Aladdin. No sooner had Aladdin heard that he must not look at the Princess than he wanted to do so. He ran ahead of the royal procession and hid behind the door of the bath house.

Soldiers approached. Maid servants approached. Finally the princess herself shimmered through the doorway in her lovely clothes. Thinking no strangers were present, Princess Buddir removed her veil and Aladdin was able to see her beautiful face.

He fell in love with her at once and, as soon as he could, the young man hurried home and told his mother that he had decided to marry the Emperor's daughter.

First his mother laughed, then she became worried. 'What foolishness is this, Aladdin?' she asked. 'The likes of you can never marry Princess Buddir. Why, your head might be struck from your shoulders for even thinking of it.'

However, Aladdin was not to be dissuaded. 'I have the slaves of the ring and of the lamp to help me,' he said. 'And, what's more, I have a hoard of jewels more precious than those in the whole of China.' Then he told his mother that the fruits he had picked so many years ago were really fine jewels. He begged her to put these gems on a dish and take them to the Emperor the very next day.

'Give them as a present,' said Aladdin. 'Then tell the Emperor that you have a fine son who wishes to marry Princess Buddir. He must be impressed by a family that can give away such jewels.'

Reluctantly Aladdin's mother agreed to do as he asked. The next day she put the jewels on a silver tray, covered them with a napkin and went and stood in the audience hall of the palace before the Emperor's throne. For a week she waited on the Emperor every day, but he did not speak to her. Viziers and great lords were always attended to before an unimportant woman.

At last the Emperor became curious about this persistent woman with her napkin-covered tray. He ordered her to speak.

'Son of Heaven, forgive my bold request,' whispered Aladdin's mother, shivering with fear. 'Allow me to make it, then depart, for I know you can never grant what I ask.'

The Emperor felt sorry for the frightened woman and promised not to punish her. Then Aladdin's mother said that her son wished to marry Princess Buddir and had sent a betrothal gift. At first the Emperor laughed in derision, but when he saw the jewels, he was astounded. They were finer than his own!

He spoke to his Vizier, who was his chief adviser. 'Should I agree to the marriage?' he asked.

As it happened, the Vizier wanted the Princess to marry his own son. 'Take the jewels,' he whispered, 'and tell this woman to return in three months' time to discuss the wedding details.'

So it was done and Aladdin's mother hurried home to tell her son that the Emperor had accepted the jewels. It seemed that the first steps towards the marriage of Aladdin and Princess Buddir had been successfully taken.

However, from that moment, the Vizier spent his time telling the Emperor how much more suitable it would be for the Princess to marry a man of good family, like his own son. He also gave the Emperor many fine presents and soon Aladdin's mother was forgotten. Her jewels were put in the royal collection and a date was set for the wedding of Princess Buddir and the Vizier's son.

One day, when Aladdin's mother was out shopping, she was amazed to see a procession of great lords in their finest clothes and to learn that they were on their way to the wedding of Princess Buddir. Hurrying home, she told Aladdin that they had been betrayed and that Princess Buddir was about to marry another man.

Filled with anger, Aladdin rubbed the lamp and summoned its slave. 'What is your wish, oh Master?' asked the genie. 'I serve whoever holds the lamp.'

'The Emperor has betrayed me,' said Aladdin. 'He is marrying his daughter to the Vizier's son this very day. Tonight, as soon as they retire to bed, bring them both here to stand before me.'

The genie bowed. 'Your wish is my command,' he boomed in his deep, echoing voice, and then he disappeared.

Back at the palace, the wedding feast drew to its close. The bride and bridegroom were taken to their bedchamber, but no sooner was the door shut, than the astonished couple found themselves magically transported to Aladdin's home.

'Take the bridegroom away and keep him prisoner until dawn,' ordered Aladdin, and the genie obeyed.

Aladdin turned to the terrified Princess. He told her of her father's deceit. He explained to her that she was his own promised bride and that he could not allow her to marry another man. Then he drew a scimitar and placed it between the Princess and himself. 'No harm will come to you,' he said. 'Tomorrow morning you will be taken back to the Emperor's palace.'

At the first light of dawn the genie brought the shivering bridegroom before Aladdin. The unfortunate young man had spent the night outside Aladdin's chamber, wearing only a night shirt. He was frozen through. 'Take the two of them back to the palace,' ordered Aladdin.

As suddenly as they had been taken away, the Princess and her bridegroom found themselves back in their bridal chamber. The Princess told her father what had happened. The bridegroom told his father, the Vizier. The next night the same thing happened, and the third. The Emperor consulted the Vizier. It was clear to them both that the marriage was doomed from the start, and it was annulled.

Meanwhile, three months had passed since Aladdin's mother had visited the Emperor to discuss the marriage of her son and the Princess Buddir. Again she went to the palace. She bowed before the Emperor and asked if he had given consideration to plans for the wedding.

The Emperor became impatient. He had been glad enough to take the jewels as a present, but he didn't want to see any more of this low-born woman. Again he consulted his Vizier.

'Make conditions for the marriage that this woman cannot possibly fulfil,' advised the Vizier. 'Then you will have kept your promise, but the affair will be over.'

The Emperor turned and smiled at Aladdin's mother. 'I must have proof that your son can support my daughter in royal state.' he said. 'Tell him to send me forty trays made of solid gold. Each tray must be piled with jewels and carried by a beautiful slave,

magnificently dressed. If your son can send me these things, then he may marry my daughter.'

Aladdin's mother bowed and left, and the Emperor smiled, thinking he would never see her again. However, after he had spoken to his mother, Aladdin withdrew to his chamber and took up the magic lamp. He rubbed it and in a moment the genie of the lamp was standing before him. 'What is your wish, oh Master?' he asked. 'I obey whoever holds the lamp.'

Aladdin told the genie what the Emperor had said, and that same day a procession of forty magnificently dressed slaves, each carrying a solid gold tray laden with precious jewels, walked to the Emperor's palace. Crowds rushed to watch and the Emperor was astounded. He sent for Aladdin to be brought before him.

Wearing the most magnificent clothes that the genie of the lamp could supply, Aladdin walked into the Emperor's palace. By this time, the Emperor was eager to welcome such a rich son-in-law into the family. The marriage contract was drawn up and the wedding ceremony was arranged for the next day.

Then Aladdin looked from a window of the palace and said to the Emperor, 'Grant me the use of the land that lies in front of us, most noble father, and I will build a palace the like of which has never been seen before. I will live there with your daughter.'

Greedy to see even more riches appear before him, the Emperor nodded. So Aladdin instructed the genie to build, in one night, a palace lined with marble, jasper and agate. The walls were built with bricks of gold and silver alternately. The windows and doors were studded with diamonds and rubies and emeralds.

The Emperor was delighted. The wedding took place and Aladdin lived happily with his Princess in the lovely palace for several years.

Far away in Africa, the sorcerer regretted his hastiness in giving up the magic lamp so easily. He decided to make another attempt to find it and once more travelled to China. Entering the city where Aladdin lived, the sorcerer soon heard tales of the rich Prince Aladdin who was married to Princess Buddir, and who lived in a palace the like of which had never been seen before.

The sorcerer hurried to the palace and after one look knew that this must be the work of the genie of the lamp. He returned to the inn where he was staying and shut himself quietly in his room. Using his magic powers he learned that the lamp was kept on a shelf in Aladdin's bedroom in the palace.

Smiling happily to himself, the sorcerer visited a coppersmith and bought a dozen new copper lamps. He disguised himself as a poor streetseller and waited by the gates of Aladdin's palace. Soon after dawn, Aladdin rode out with his men for a day's hunting.

When he was safely out of sight, the sorcerer strolled under the windows of the palace calling, 'New lamps for old. I give new lamps for old. Who would like a new lamp for an old one?'

The street urchins laughed at hearing such a strange cry. Several of them hastened home and came back with chipped old lamps, and the sorcerer gave them shiny, new, copper ones in return. A maidservant, looking from a window of the palace, saw what was happening and ran to tell Princess Buddir.

'An old man is out in the street offering to give new lamps for old,' she laughed. 'Did anyone ever see such a foolish thing before?'

'It cannot be true,' said the Princess.

Then she remembered the old lamp that Aladdin kept in his bedroom. 'Fetch that old lamp from your master's room and offer that to the old man,' she said. 'See if he will give us a nice new lamp for that old thing.'

The maidservant took the magic lamp and carried it into the street. 'Will you give me a new lamp for this?' she asked.

The sorcerer's heart leaped for joy. 'Willingly, my dear,' he replied and, giving the girl a new lamp, he thankfully clasped the magic lamp to his chest and hurried back to his room at the inn.

As soon as he was alone, he rubbed the lamp and at once the genie appeared. 'What is your wish, oh Master?' he asked. 'I serve whoever holds the lamp.'

'Take me and Aladdin's palace and everything in it back to my home in Africa,' said the sorcerer. 'And do it now.'

'To hear is to obey, oh Master,' said the genie.

At once Aladdin's palace, with the Princess and servants in it, disappeared from its place next to the Emperor's palace and was transported to Africa. The Emperor, happening to glance from his window to admire his daughter's home, rubbed his eyes in astonishment. He sent for the Vizier and the grounds of the palace were searched, but no trace of the palace could be found.

The Emperor was furious and ordered Aladdin to be put to death. However, the common people who loved Aladdin for his generosity towards them, rose in rebellion and the Emperor was forced to think again. Aladdin was dragged before him.

'Bring my daughter back safely within forty days,' said the Emperor, 'or I shall have you hunted down and killed.'

Aladdin was thrown out into the streets of the city, with nothing to help him. Weak and hungry, Aladdin stumbled and fell down a rough slope. As he fell, he rubbed his hand along the ground. In so doing, he rubbed the ring that the sorcerer had given him at the entrance to the underground cavern.

At once the genie of the ring stood before him. 'I serve whoever wears the ring,' said the genie. 'What is your wish, oh Master?'

Almost weeping for joy, Aladdin asked the genie to bring back his palace and the Princess to their rightful home.

The genie shook his head. 'I am the genie of the ring, not the genie of the lamp,' he said. 'My powers are not so great. I cannot bring your palace here, but I can take you to it, if you wish.'

'Yes it is,' Aladdin said, and immediately he found himself outside his palace, that was now standing on a plain in Africa, not far from a big city.

Aladdin saw that he was beneath the windows of the rooms of Princess Buddir, his wife. By chance a servant girl looked from one of the windows just then and was overjoyed to see Aladdin standing below. She let him in by a small side door and soon Aladdin and the Princess were in each other's arms.

After many tears and much talk the Princess learned that she had been the cause of her own misfortune in giving the old lamp to the streetseller. Aladdin guessed that the streetseller was the sorcerer he had met so many years before and learned, in his turn, that the sorcerer kept the magic lamp tucked in his jacket, where no one but he could touch it.

'Do not give up hope,' Aladdin said to Buddir. 'We will outwit this wicked man yet.' And he slipped out of the palace again.

So that his strange Chinese attire might not attract attention, Aladdin persuaded a poor passer by to exchange clothes with him. Then he walked into the nearby town and found the shop that sold potions. He pulled a well-filled purse from his pocket and asked for a small bottle of a certain drug.

The bottle was soon in his hands. He hurried back to the palace and crept silently up to the Princess's rooms. 'At supper tonight,' he said, 'smile and sing for the sorcerer. Then ask him to drink your health in a cup of wine – he will do it to please you. This potion will be in the wine. As soon as it has passed his lips, he will fall into an endless sleep. When this happens, send one of your women to fetch me.'

The brave Buddir did as Aladdin instructed. Although she hated the evil sorcerer, she ordered her servants to sing for him and smiled and laughed at his words. When she asked him to toast her health in a glass of wine, the sorcerer drained it to the last drop. Then he fell back and never woke again.

'Quick. Fetch my husband,' ordered the Princess, and her most trusted servant hastened to fetch Aladdin. He came quickly and ordered the Princess and her maids to wait quietly outside.

When he was alone with the sorcerer, he bent over him and pulled the magic lamp out of his jacket. He rubbed the lamp and the genie appeared. 'Your wish is my command, oh Master,' said the genie. 'I serve whoever holds the lamp.'

'Leave this sorcerer to sleep in the desert,' said Aladdin. 'But transport the palace and everyone in it back to our home in China.' There was one gentle bump as the palace left the ground, and another as it landed, and that was all anyone felt of the long journey home.

The Emperor, still griefstricken by the loss of his daughter, was looking from a window when, to his amazement, he saw Aladdin's palace reappear. He ran down to the jewelled entrance doors and embraced his dear child. Then he begged Aladdin to forgive him for the harsh way he had treated him.

'There is nothing to forgive,' replied Aladdin, 'for you simply did your duty.'

After that Aladdin took great care that the magic lamp never left his sight and they were never troubled by the sorcerer again. When the Emperor died, Aladdin and the Princess ruled China jointly and lived long and happy lives together.

4

Joseph who Dreamed the Truth

The adventures of Joseph, in his coat of many colours is one of the best-loved stories in The Bible. It belongs with the traditional tales of the Middle East, where Jacob and his sons lived thousands of years ago.

Long ago, a rich man called Jacob lived in the land of Canaan. He had many flocks and many wives and children. However, the son that he loved best was called Joseph. Jacob loved Joseph so much that he could not help favouring him more than his other children. Joseph's brothers, the sons of Jacob's other wives, became jealous of the boy who, it seemed, could do no wrong.

When Joseph was fifteen, his father gave him a coat of many colours. This was a great luxury for a shepherd boy. The other sons looked at Joseph, handsome in his elegant coat, and were more envious than ever.

Joseph himself did not help the situation. He had unfortunate dreams that were so vivid he could not shake them from his mind when he woke. 'Brothers, listen to me,' he said. 'Last night I dreamed that we were binding sheaves in the field. My sheaf stood tall and straight, but the sheaves made by the rest of you drooped over and bowed before mine.'

His brothers were not pleased. 'So, being preferred to us in life is not enough,' they scowled. 'We must bow down before you in your dreams as well.'

Unfortunately, Joseph went on having these powerful dreams, and with the tactlessness of youth continued to talk about them. 'Father,' he said, standing before Jacob, 'last night I dreamed that the sun and the moon and eleven stars knelt before me.'

Much as Jacob loved Joseph, he felt it was unseemly talk from a young boy. 'If you are trying to say that, because of this dream, your family and I should kneel before you, then that is not right,' said Jacob. 'Do not talk in such a way, Joseph.'

Although Jacob rebuked Joseph, he took note of the strange dreams and wondered if his dear son was destined for greatness.

Time went by and Jacob's flocks were feeding in the land of Shechem. Jacob became anxious for their welfare and sent Joseph to find them. 'Find your brothers, who are looking after my animals,' instructed Jacob. 'See if all is well with them and with the flocks. Then come home to me.'

After days of searching, Joseph found the flocks in the land of Dothan. His brothers saw him approaching in his bright coat from a long way off. 'Here he comes,' they said, 'doubtless with more dreams to tell us how high and mighty he is!'

The brothers looked around and saw that they were far from home and in a lonely place. 'This is a good spot in which to rid ourselves of our beloved little brother,' they said. 'Let's kill Joseph and tell Father that the wild animals took him. How will anyone at home ever know that we are not telling the truth?'

Fortunately for Joseph, one of his brothers, called Reuben, was more compassionate than the others. 'He is only a boy!' said Reuben. 'We cannot kill him. Remember he is the son of our father. We don't want his blood on our hands.'

Still the other brothers wanted to kill Joseph. Reuben pleaded with them: unlike the others, he did not hate his young brother. 'Throw him in that pit,' he begged. 'He will die, but at least you will not have shed his blood.'

The other brothers agreed to this and Reuben was content because he intended to creep back later and rescue Joseph.

A little while later Joseph arrived at his brothers' camp with the messages from home, hoping for a friendly greeting and food and drink. Instead his coat of many colours was dragged from his back and he was flung into a deep pit. Satisfied with the revenge they had taken on the young dreamer, the brothers sat down to eat, while Reuben went out to check the flocks.

Not long afterwards some Ishmaelite traders came riding by. This gave one of the brothers an idea. 'Let's sell Joseph to the Ishmaelites,' he said. That way we will get rid of him without killing him, and make some money as well.'

Joseph was sold to the Ishmaelites for twenty pieces of silver and taken away to Egypt. By the time Reuben returned from checking the flocks, the merchants had gone. There was little hope of finding them.

Reuben looked into the empty pit and was beside himself with grief. He wept and tore his clothes and shouted to his brothers,

'The boy is gone. Where is he? What have you done with him?'

The brothers laughed and said, 'He is gone and that is all there is to it.' They killed a baby goat and spilled its blood all over Joseph's coat of many colours. When the grass was all cropped and they drove their flocks home, they took it with them and showed it to Jacob.

'We found this near our flocks,' they said. 'Surely it is the coat that you gave to our brother, Joseph?'

Jacob looked at the blood-stained coat in horror. 'I did send Joseph to find you,' he said. 'This is his coat. A wild beast has killed my dearest boy.' Then Jacob tore his clothes and put on sackcloth. Nobody could comfort him for his heart was broken.

Taken south into Egypt, Joseph was sold as a slave to Potiphar, an important man who was captain of the guard to the Pharaoh, the ruler of Egypt. Now Joseph was an intelligent boy, who grew up to be a charming young man. Potiphar found that all the tasks he gave to Joseph were well done. As the years went by, Joseph became manager of the entire household. Potiphar had nothing to worry about, while Joseph lived a rich life, dressed in fine clothes. I am a slave, but God has smiled on me, Joseph thought.

However, Potiphar's wife was discontented. The household was managed by Joseph and Potiphar was often away on army service. Potiphar's wife felt bored and neglected. She looked at Joseph's handsome face and fell in love. Joseph knew only too well that such a love could bring nothing but disaster to him. He avoided his master's wife and she took offence. Her love turned to fury, so when Potiphar camed home, she told him a pack of lies.

'Joseph is in love with me,' she said. 'He keeps pestering me. I am not safe in the house while you are away. He has betrayed the great trust you place in him.'

51

Joseph was thrown into prison. His days of fine clothes and good food were over. He was thirty years old and it was thirteen years since his brothers had sold him. However, Joseph was a man who always made the best of things. His faith in God was strong and he busied himself helping those around him. Soon Joseph was managing affairs in prison, as he had managed Potiphar's household. The prison governor trusted Joseph and all the arrangements inside the prison walls were left to him. Yet, despite the governor's trust, Joseph was still a prisoner.

Time went by and one day the Pharaoh's butler and baker were sent to prison. The two men were terrified at having offended the Pharaoh and they dreamed strange dreams.

'What can these dreams mean?' they said to one another. 'If only we were free and could speak to an interpreter of dreams, we might learn what our fates will be.'

Joseph said to them, 'God is the giver of all dreams. Tell your dreams to me and God will tell me their meaning.'

Eagerly the two men babbled out their stories. 'In my dream,' said the butler, 'I was standing in front of a vine. The vine had three shoots. They budded and came into blossom and bore fruit quickly, while I watched. Then I picked the fruit and put it into the Pharaoh's cup that suddenly appeared in my hand. Then the Pharaoh was before me and I leaned forward and gave him the cup of fruit.' The butler looked anxiously at Joseph. 'What does all that mean?' he asked.

Joseph said, 'The three shoots were three days. In three days the Pharaoh will free you and take you back to the palace and you will serve him his food, as you used to do.'

The butler sighed with relief. 'Oh, I am so thankful,' he said.

'Then,' said Joseph, 'when you are free, remember me still in prison. Try to obtain my release.'

Then the baker told his dream, hoping for an equally good interpretation. 'I dreamed that I had three white baskets on my head,' he said. 'The top basket was full of pieces of food for the Pharaoh to eat, but before I could give them to him, birds from the air swooped down and ate them.'

Joseph looked at him sadly. 'The three baskets are three days,' he said, 'but the meaning of your dream is that, in three days, the Pharaoh will lift your head from your shoulders and hang up your body, and the birds of the air will come and devour you.'

The baker sank into gloom.

On the third day, as Joseph had foreseen, the baker was beheaded and the fortunate butler was restored to his position in the Pharaoh's palace. However the butler immediately forgot his companions in the prison and did nothing to help Joseph.

For two more years Joseph stayed in prison. Then the Pharaoh himself had a puzzling and disturbing dream. He dreamed that he was standing beside the river Nile. Seven fat cows came up out of the water and ate the grass in a meadow. Then seven more cows came up from the river. They were lean and diseased. The lean cows ate up the fat cows. Then the Pharaoh woke.

The next night the Pharaoh had another vivid dream. In this dream seven ears of corn grew on one stalk. They were fat and good. Then at their side, seven thin, shrivelled ears of corn sprang from the ground. The east wind began to blow. The seven thin ears of corn ate the seven fat ears. Then the Pharaoh woke.

The dreams had been so real and so alarming that the Pharaoh called together all the magicians of Egypt and asked them what the dreams could mean. No one could tell him. The Pharaoh became more and more agitated and everyone in the palace was afraid of his bad temper. Suddenly the butler remembered Joseph. Hoping to gain favour with the Pharaoh, the butler told him that there was a young Hebrew man in the prison who had correctly interpreted dreams for him and the baker.

Everyone in the prison was surprised when the Pharaoh ordered Joseph to be brought before him. Joseph shaved and the prison governor gave him new clothes, so that he might look presentable to appear before the ruler of all Egypt.

'I have had two dreams,' the Pharaoh said to Joseph. He told him about the cows and the corn. 'I have told all this to my magicians, but none can explain them. Do you know what my dreams mean?'

Joseph said to the Pharaoh, 'The dreams are one. They have the same meaning. God is telling you what is about to happen. The seven fat cows and the seven fat ears of corn are seven good years. The seven lean cows and the seven withered ears of corn are seven years of famine. This is the message that God is sending to you. For seven years there will be plenty in Egypt. The crops will be rich and food will be abundant. Then will come seven years of bad harvests and famine. All the good years will be forgotten and there will be hunger and death. God has sent the dream twice to assure you that these things really will happen.'

Joseph paused to collect his thoughts. Then he continued, 'As God has seen fit to send this warning, then you should choose a man with the wisdom and skill to manage Egypt's affairs. Give him officials to help him and during the seven good years, let this man take a fifth of the food and store it in preparation for the seven lean years. Let food be stored in the cities for all the people who live there and in the countryside for when the crops fail.'

The Pharaoh and his court thought that this was wise advice. So the Pharaoh said, 'Joseph, since God has revealed all these things to you, then you are the man who must prepare us against the seven years of famine.'

He ordered that Joseph should be put in charge of the royal household and that everyone, save only the Pharaoh himself, should obey him. He gave him a ring for his finger and a gold chain for his neck. Then he gave him one of his best chariots in which to drive. Finally he gave him an Egyptian name and an Egyptian wife. Joseph had command over the land of Egypt.

Everything happened as the dreams foretold. For seven years the harvests were good. Food was plentiful and Joseph gathered in stores of corn. In the eighth year the crops failed and there were seven lean years. The people who lived in Egypt were fortunate. When the shops in the towns were empty of corn, and when the farmers could no longer reap crops from their fields, they were able to buy corn from Joseph's stores. They could survive and pray for the seven years of hardship to pass.

Outside Egypt people were starving. After two of the seven lean years had gone by, Jacob and his family were short of food and beginning to get desperate. Hearing that there was corn in Egypt,

Jacob sent ten of his sons with pack animals to buy corn and bring it home. But Jacob would not send his youngest son, Benjamin. Benjamin was Joseph's full brother, the only other son of Joseph's mother. After Joseph's disappearance so many years before, Benjamin, who had just been born became Jacob's best-loved son, as Joseph had been.

'I will not send Benjamin on this journey,' said Jacob. 'He might come to harm. My heart must not be broken again.'

The hungry brothers made the long trek down to Egypt and asked the way to the food stores, where Joseph was supervising the selling of corn to foreigners. During his many years in Egypt, Joseph had not only grown into a man, but he dressed and spoke like an Egyptian. His Egyptian wife had borne him two sons, whom he loved dearly. His new family now filled his life. His old father and jealous brothers were a distant memory.

One day, as he was going about his work, Joseph turned to find his brothers standing before him. Suddenly he remembered his old life as though it was only yesterday. He was overcome with homesickness and longing for his own people. However, he could not forgive these men who had sold him into slavery. He was filled with hatred for them and determined to make them suffer.

'You are not genuine buyers,' he said to them harshly. 'You are thieves. You have come to spy on our stores, then you will rob us.'

The brothers did not recognise Joseph in his aristocratic clothes and rich jewels. They were terrified by his sudden rage. They protested that they were innocent and hastened to explain that they were the twelve sons of Jacob, an honest herdsman.

Joseph seized on their words. 'Twelve sons?' he said. 'There are only ten of you. Your story does not hang together. You must be spies!'

The brothers all spoke at once. They told him about Benjamin, the only full brother of a brother called Joseph who had died as a boy. They told him how Benjamin was their father's best-loved son and that was why he had not been allowed to make the journey. Joseph learned for the first time that he had a young brother. He longed to see him.

'I will sell you corn to take back to your family only if you promise to return with your brother,' he said. 'I will keep one of you here in Egypt. He will be released when you return with Benjamin.'

This did not please the brothers. They knew that their father would never let Benjamin go. Not expecting Joseph to understand

their tribal language, they spoke to each other in front of him.

'Which of us will be left here?' they asked. 'When will he be released? Why is this Egyptian official being so difficult with us? He is not troubling any of the other foreigners buying corn.'

Then Reuben spoke. 'It is a judgement on us,' he said. 'All those years ago, I tried to stop you from harming Joseph. This is God's revenge for our wickedness to our brother.'

Hearing the brothers talking in his childhood language upset Joseph. Suddenly his Egyptian friends and even his Egyptian family seemed like strangers. He turned aside and wept. Then, with his heart still hard against his brothers, he took one, called Simeon, and put him in prison. He ordered his steward to fill their sacks with corn as they asked and give them food for the journey home. He also secretly put the money the brothers had paid for the corn into their sacks.

The brothers hastened on their way, reluctantly leaving Simeon behind. On the road home they discovered that their money had been given back to them and they were afraid. Why had they been treated in such a strange way? They had been spoken to harshly, and yet they had been given the corn free. The whole thing must be a trick to get them into more trouble.

Jacob listened to his sons' story when they returned and shook his head. 'I will not send Benjamin to a man who behaves in such a strange way,' he said. 'I would never see the boy again and my grief would send me to the grave.'

So the brothers stayed at home. Simeon remained in prison in Egypt and two more years went by.

Still the crops failed and still the famine raged. The time came when all the corn the brothers had brought from Egypt was eaten up. 'Go to Egypt and buy more corn,' said Jacob.

The brothers would not go. They remembered the strange conduct of the rich official who had command of all the food and was second only to the Pharaoh.

'We must take Benjamin with us or we dare not go,' they said.

Jacob became impatient. 'Why did you have to tell the man you had another brother?' he asked. 'If you had not told him about Benjamin, we would not be in this trouble.'

'But he questioned us,' replied the brothers. 'He asked us about our father and if we had any other brothers. How were we to know he would ask to see Benjamin? Why should anyone in Egypt care about him? How could we have expected it?'

At last starvation forced Jacob to let Benjamin go to Egypt. He insisted that his sons took not only money for the second purchase of corn, but also the money that had been returned to them the first time. 'Whether it was a mistake, or whether it was a trick, it is best to take the money we owe,' he said.

The brothers also took a present for the official, hoping that they might win the friendship of this unpredictable man. With fear and worry in their hearts, they set out.

Again the brothers stood before Joseph. Again they asked for corn. They held out their gift and double money for the corn, explaining that the money for the first supply of corn had been returned to them. Then they pointed to Benjamin standing with them and asked for Simeon to be released.

Joseph looked at Benjamin, his own full brother, and his heart was filled with joy. Leaping to his feet, he told his servants to take all the brothers to his house and he ordered a great feast to be prepared. The brothers were treated as important guests. Joseph was friendly and asked for news of their home and father. But the brothers were still afraid. Why were they being treated in such a special way? they wondered.

Joseph told his steward to give the brothers all the corn they wanted, and, as before, to put the purchase money into the sacks of corn. He also told him to put a silver cup into Benjamin's sack.

'After these men have left for home,' Joseph ordered, 'ride after them. Search the sack and find the silver cup and ask them why they have stolen it.'

The brothers stood before Joseph again, this time accused of

theft. Joseph said that he would pardon them, but Benjamin must stay behind with him as his servant because the cup had been found in Benjamin's sack. In this way Joseph hoped to keep his dear brother with him. However, one of the brothers, called Judah, stepped forward and, not caring that Joseph was the most important man in Egypt after the Pharaoh, explained that they could not possibly return to Jacob without Benjamin.

'After the loss of his other son, Joseph, my father has loved this boy,Benjamin, most of all,' said Judah. 'If we return without Benjamin, my father will die of grief. Keep me, but let the boy go.'

Joseph could keep his secret no longer. He ordered his servants to leave the room and he said to his brothers, 'Don't you know me? I am Joseph.'

They were puzzled. 'I am your brother Joseph, whom you sold as a slaveto the Ishmaelites,' said the strange Egyptian official in their own language.

The brothers stared at him and at last recognised the features of their brother in the face of the mature man.

Seeing their fear, Joseph said, 'Do not be frightened. I see now that this was the work of God. He caused me to be sent into Egypt, so that I could store the corn and save my family from destruction. God has made me second to the Pharaoh and the ruler in Egypt. Now go home to my father and tell him that Joseph lives. Tell him that I am rich and powerful. Tell him to come to me with all his children and his children's children and his flocks and herds, and I will care for him. He shall have grazing land in the north of Egypt.'

Now, in the eyes of the Pharaoh, Joseph could do no wrong because he had saved the land from famine and also made the Pharaoh very rich from the sale of corn. The Pharaoh agreed that Joseph's family could live in Egypt and sent many waggons to make the journey more comfortable for the women and the young children.

When Jacob heard that Joseph lived, his heart was filled with joy. The old man came to Egypt with his family. As they arrived, Joseph rode out in his chariot to meet his father. They fell into each other's arms and wept. And Jacob said, 'Now when death comes for me, I shall die a happy man, for I have seen that you, my dearest son, are alive and well.'

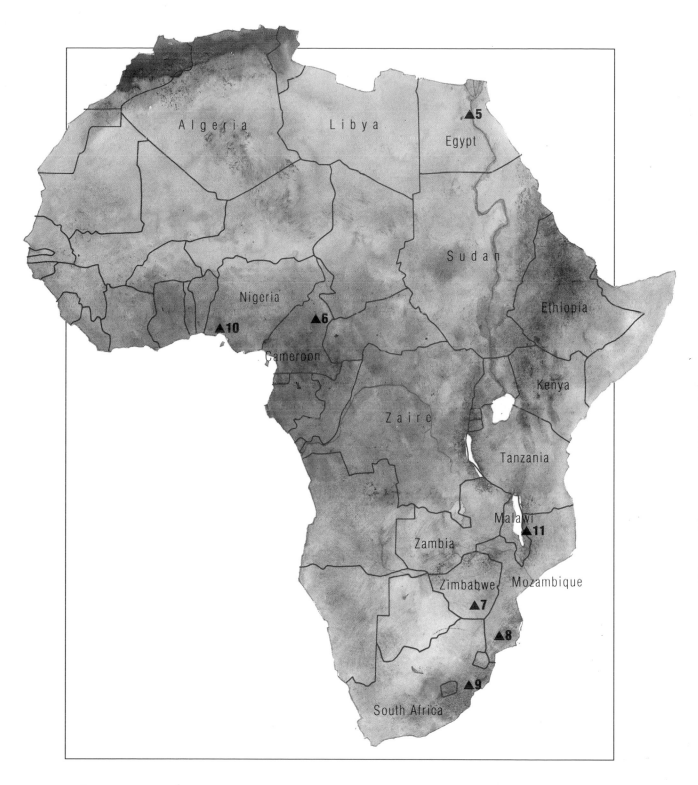

Africa

5 The Battles of Horus

6 The Cunning Monkey

7 The Story of Untombinde

8 The Horns of Plenty

9 The Proud Princess

10 Tricky Mr Rabbit

11 The Cunning Man

5

The Battles of Horus

Egypt lies at the north-east corner of Africa, straddling the profitable trade routes between Europe, India and the Far East. The traditional tales of Egypt feature a bewildering array of gods. At one time, each of the local districts had its own 'company' of nine gods and each had their own legends. In some districts, Ra, Horus, Atum, Harmachus and Khepra are all names for the one Sun God. In others, Horus is the son or grandson of Ra and the other names refer to different Sun Gods. In the following story, Horus is clearly the grandson of Ra and the plot seems to be a chronicle of ancient tribal conflicts.

Long ago when the world was young, Horus was the warrior god of the daytime sky. At dawn, Horus was a young and eager boy, like the sun's first rays. At midday, Horus was a man with the full strength of the sun. Sometimes he appeared with the body of a man and the head of a falcon, sometimes he was a golden, raging lion. As the sun sank towards the west, the power of Horus waned. This was the time for the enemies of Horus to attack him. Set, the god of the night-time sky, was the enemy of the beautiful god of daytime. When night fell, it was wise for Horus to be wary.

Now Ra, the god of the sun, was growing old. His enemies attacked the borders of his kingdom of Lower (or northern) Egypt, taking land here, stealing goods and horses there.

Set was his greatest enemy, for Set was a cunning warrior. He ruled over Upper (or southern) Egypt and had many evil followers. Set had killed Osiris, son of Ra and father of Horus. This deed could never be forgotten or forgiven, for Osiris had been much loved by his family.

Ra marched south with his army into Nubia, where he was met by his grandson Horus, at the head of another army.

'Grandfather,' said Horus, 'your enemies are marching against you. They will not disappear like water in the desert and they are cunning and bold.'

The old god, Ra, looked at his strong, golden grandson. 'Take your place at the head of our armies,' he said. 'Go forth and trample our enemies into the dust.'

Horus smiled. He was not without cunning of his own. 'There is more than one way to defeat an army,' he said.

Leaving his men in hiding, Horus went to consult Thoth, the god of wisdom. Thoth knew many spells and he gave Horus a glittering globe that shone like the sun and had great wings on either side. Horus flew into the sky and hovered over Set's armies, reflecting heat down at them so that the soldiers' minds became confused. They did not know where they were, or who they were, and they picked up their swords and slew each other. Only a handful of Set's men staggered alive from the battlefield.

Still in his golden globe with the wings on either side, Horus flew low over the dead and dying, looking for his enemy Set, but he was not there. Fortunately for Set, he had been away in the south, as he had not thought that battle was about to begin.

Horus returned to Ra and Isis, his mother and the goddess of motherhood, and told them how he had defeated Set's army. They were amazed and could scarcely believe his words because they knew that their own armies had not unsheathed a single sword.

Horus took Ra and Isis into the golden globe and flew with them over their dead enemies so that they could see for themselves. The old man was happy. 'Now I am safe,' he smiled.

Ra invited Horus to take a boat ride with him and his court on the cool waters of the Nile, but they were rejoicing too soon. Set had more followers who were eager to overthrow the power of Ra.

'Horus is not the only one to know cunning tricks,' said Set. He turned his followers into crocodiles and hippopotamuses and sent them into the River Nile. 'Turn the boats over and swallow

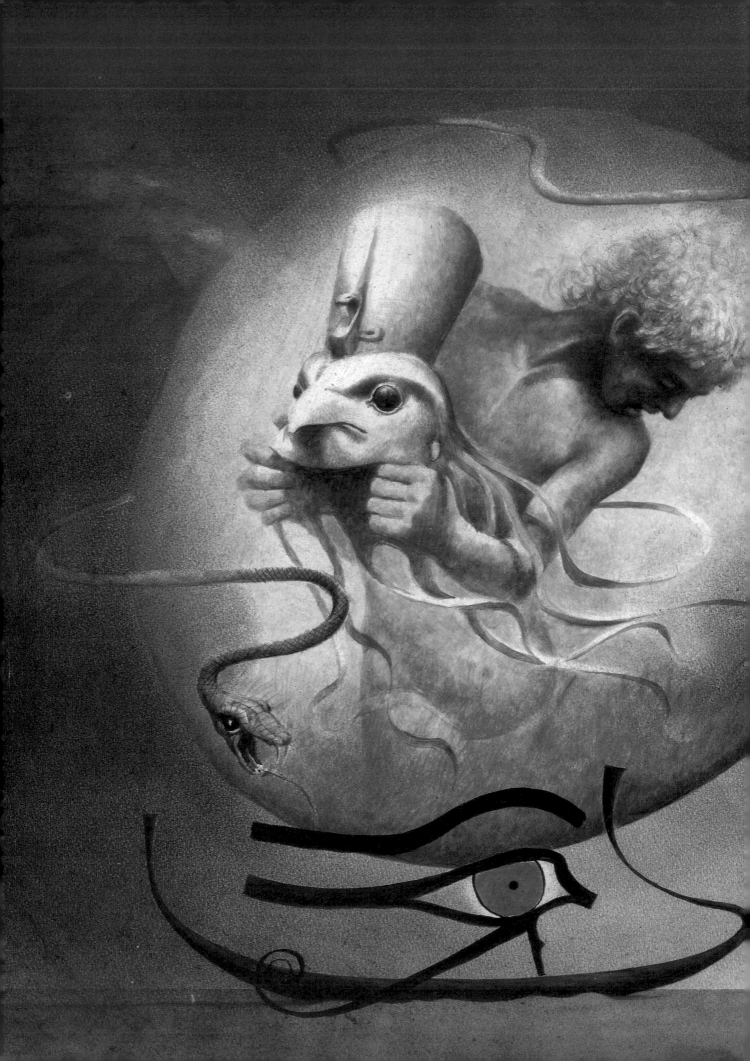

Ra and Horus,' he ordered. 'No harm will come to you. Your thick hides will protect you.'

Set's followers slipped into the river ahead of the boats of Ra and Horus, but Thoth, the god of wisdom, sent a warning to his friends. He also sent more of his magical weapons, equipping Horus and his men with spears and chains of glittering metal.

The army of crocodiles and hippopotamuses charged at the oncoming boats, churning up the water. Horus spoke the words taught to him by Thoth from his Book of Magic, while his men

stabbed into the water with their glittering magical weapons. Many of the crocodiles were killed. Many hippopotamuses were captured. Many more fled. The animals that fled to the south escaped, but Horus pursued those that swam northwards. He overtook them and, after another great battle, slew even more of the followers of Set, the god of night.

These great victories pleased Ra, but still the old man was frightened. 'I shall never be safe while Set and his followers live,' he said. 'Horus, climb into your golden globe with the huge wings on either side and slay the rest of my enemies.'

Horus, the great warrior, was eager to obey these instructions. He entered the golden globe and this time the goddesses Nekhebet and Uazet flew on either side. Thoth, the god of wisdom, joined Ra in the boats and they sailed south, while Horus and the vulture-headed Nekhebet and Uazet, the cobra goddess, flew above them. They scanned the water but the crocodiles and hippopotamuses had learned a bitter lesson and stayed under water, out of sight.

For days Ra and Horus searched for their enemies. The goddesses Nekhebet and Uazet twisted and curled through the sky in the shape of snakes. At last they saw the crocodiles and hippopotamuses lurking beneath the surface of the Nile. Calling Horus in his golden globe, they reflected heat down at the creatures under the waves. Those that did not swim away were destroyed. Ra watched from his boat and rejoiced.

Then Horus called for his soldiers and drove the remnants of Set's army from the land. Throughout all the battles, Horus searched for Set, wishing to fight him with his own hands in revenge for killing Osiris. It was not to be. Set escaped.

Time passed. Ra and Horus thought that the danger was over. Then one morning, as the boy Horus came up with the dawn and grew to manhood at midday, Set stepped forward and challenged him to a fight to the death. It was agreed that the fight should take place on the River Nile. Isis, the grieving widow of Osiris, gave her son Horus a magical boat. This lovely craft was not only decorated from bow to stern, it was also protected by ancient spells so no harm could come to anyone who sailed in it.

Set took the shape of a great red hippopotamus and slipped into the water to lie in wait. Then he called up a great storm to rage along the river. Huge waves lashed the boats of Horus and his followers. Only the magic of Isis saved them from sinking. All the while Set lurked on the riverbed, waiting to swallow the drowning bodies of his enemies.

Realising that the power of the storm was not enough to carry out his plans, Set, the god of the night, caused darkness to fill the sky. 'The power of Horus will falter without the sun's rays,' he smiled.

However, the Horus's courage did not fail. A great light like the sun shone from the prow of his boat and cut through the darkness. Horus grew to the size of a giant, and peered out into the storm looking for his enemy. He had another magical gift from Thoth – a harpoon sharp enough to pierce the strongest defence.

Set, disguised as a red hippopotamus, lurked beneath the surface of the water, waiting impatiently for the ship to sink so that he could swallow Horus. At last, puzzled to know why the ship stayed afloat, Set raised his head into the light shining from the prow of the magical boat. One glimpse of his enemy was enough for the mighty warrior of the sun. Horus threw the harpoon into Set's head and killed him.

The storm ceased to rage. The river became calm. Horus and his companions sailed back to stand before Ra, the mighty god.

'Grandfather,' said Horus, 'Set, your enemy, is killed. At last the murder of Osiris is avenged.' Then there was great rejoicing throughout the land and many songs were sung to glorify Horus, the mighty warrior.

6

The Clever Monkey

This story is told by the people who live on the west coast of Africa. Tricky Mr Rabbit *comes from the same area.*

Once there were two cats who were very fond of eating cheese. One fine day, when the women were busy talking together, the cats stole some cheese. Then came the problem of dividing it into equal shares. The cats eyed one another suspiciously, each thinking that the other would take the bigger portion.

At last one cat said, 'Let us ask a monkey to divide the cheese for us.' The other agreed willingly and they approached a monkey, who just as willingly took the cheese.

'Fetch some scales,' the monkey said to the two cats.

When the cats returned, the monkey took a knife and cut the cheese into two pieces. However, one piece was clearly much bigger than the other.

'Dear me!' said the monkey. 'This will never do. I will eat part of the big piece of cheese to make it weigh the same as the other.'

Before the cats could object, the monkey ate part of the cheese and, of course, he ate too much.

'Dear me!' he said. 'Now this piece is smaller. I shall have to eat some of the other cheese to make the two pieces the same size.'

By this time the cats realised that the monkey intended to eat all the cheese. 'Please do not bother with it any more,' they said. 'Give the cheese back to us and we will divide it ourselves.'

The monkey continued to nibble at the cheese.

'I could not do that,' he said. 'You would start quarrelling again for sure. Then the king of all the animals would blame me for the conflict between you. No, I must continue to bite first this piece of cheese and then that piece, until they are exactly the same weight. If all the cheese is eaten in the course of my efforts, then that is fate and you must accept it.'

The cats saw that the cheese would never be returned to them and turned away in disgust.

The monkey laughed and called after them, 'You have learned a good lesson. Never let greed lead you into foolishness.'

Then he finished enjoying the cheese.

7

The Story of Untombinde

_This, and the following two stories, are told by the Zulu and
Sesuto tribes of southern Africa. Like many of the stories from
this area, they are serious, reflecting the dignity of successful
warrior tribes.
The tribal lands were good cattle country with green pastures,
and stories about rich kings with many wives were often told._

Long ago, near the boundaries of a great kingdom, there was a haunted pool. A monster lived in the depths of the pool and brave men were afraid to go there. Untombinde, the daughter of the King, was tall and beautiful and knew no fear. She had heard that the waters of this pool glittered like precious stones and tasted richer than the finest milk. Untombinde wished to go there.

One year when many rains had fallen and all the rivers were full, Untombinde asked if she might visit the pool. Her parents forbade her to go. For a year Untombinde dreamed of the waters of the haunted pool and, after the rains had fallen, she asked if she might go there. Again her parents forbade it.

Another year went by. The rains fell in abundance and for a third time Untombinde asked if she might visit the haunted pool. Her parents saw that they would enjoy no peace until they agreed, so they gave their consent.

Untombinde behaved like a girl setting out on her wedding journey. She chose two hundred village maidens to walk with her in procession and told them to sing and dance as if they were travelling to meet her bridegroom. The laughing girls formed two lines, and set out eagerly on their adventure.

Before the sun had set, the procession of girls reached the haunted pool. They were hot and tired. Pulling off their brass anklets and bracelets and their beaded skirts, the girls plunged thankfully into the cool waters. They laughed and splashed and swam in water more lovely than they had ever seen before.

As the girls left the waters of the haunted pool, one by one, they found that their clothes and ornaments had vanished. They wailed and cried. Soon all the girls, except Untombinde herself, were crying at the water's edge.

'It is all the fault of Untombinde!' shrieked one of the girls. 'She brought us to this unlucky place. Now our clothes and jewels have gone and we are cold and alone and night is falling.'

'It must be the monster of the pool who has taken our clothes,' sobbed another girl. 'We must beg his forgiveness for disturbing the peace of his home. We must beg him to return our clothes.'

One by one the girls knelt down and shrieked and wailed for forgiveness. One by one the clothes and ornaments of each girl were restored. Only Untombinde stood tall with her head held high and refused to beg for forgiveness. 'I am a beautiful princess admired by all. I will never beg before a monster,' she said.

Her speech so angered the monster that he seized Untombinde and dragged her below the surface of the pool where he swallowed her. The girls fled in terror back to their kraal, their village, and told the King and his wife what had happened.

'This is terrible,' gasped the King. 'I knew no good could come of going to that haunted place. Now I shall never see my lovely daughter again.'

Then the King called his young warriors and told them that he wanted revenge. 'Sharpen your spears. Put on your war dress!' ordered the King. 'Go to the haunted pool and slay the monster.'

The warriors obeyed the commands of their King. From far off the monster heard their feet running over the ground. He heard the rattle of their spears on their shields. He heard their battle cries and he rose from the pool to meet them. The mighty monster opened his jaws wide and swallowed every last warrior.

'Who are these people who will never leave me in peace?' groaned the monster. 'I will spoil their fields and destroy their kraal and be rid of them.'

Bowed down with the

71

weight of all the people he had eaten, the monster waddled towards the village, eating everything that lay in his path.

At the gate of the kraal, the King himself confronted the monster. By now the monster from the pool was so bloated with everything he had swallowed, that he could scarcely move.

The King stepped forward, raised his spear, and with one slash cut open the monster from throat to stomach. Immediately all the warriors and Untombinde herself fell out into the sweet air. The monster died in a pool of blood and the whole village rejoiced.

Near the kraal where Untombinde lived, were the wide lands of a great King. This King had many wives and children. However, there was one wife who had no children. Normally this wife would have been sent to live in disgrace in the poorest hut, but she was the daughter of a powerful King and her husband did not dare mistreat her. This made the other wives very jealous. They hated the childless wife and treated her unkindly whenever they could.

One day, as she so often did, the childless wife was sitting weeping by her hut, when two pigeons landed before her. They offered to give her a child in return for the seeds of the castor plant that the wife kept in her hut. Joyfully she fetched the seeds and scattered them before the pigeons. The birds ate their fill, then they pecked at the side of the woman until they drew blood.

'Now you will bear a child,' they said and flew away.

To the joy of the woman, she gave birth to a son nine months later. He was a handsome boy, and as his mother's family was so rich, the boy was made the heir to his father, and his mother was made Head Wife and Queen. At once all the other wives were filled with hatred and their children were consumed with jealousy.

The new Queen was afraid that her son might be killed by one of the other wives or children. She wrapped him in the skin of a boa constrictor and kept him hidden away. The years went by, but still the Queen kept the child hidden. People began to whisper that the boy had died or that he had turned into a snake. Still the Queen would not show her child; she was too frightened of their jealousy.

Soon people began to forget that the Queen had ever had a child. The family from which she came became poor and everyone lost their respect for this strange woman. She was sent to live in the farthest and poorest hut, as if she were indeed childless.

By this time, the boy had grown into a young man. He could not understand why he lived such a strange, secret life. At last he told his mother that he would no longer live with her.

'It is you who are making me an outcast,' he said. 'It is your fault that my brothers and sisters wish to kill me.' He left home and his mother could not find him. She could get no help or sympathy from her husband or the other wives – they thought that the child had died years before. Still, ever hopeful that one day the boy would return,his mother built a hut for him and every evening she put meat and drink inside it.

Now stories always become more interesting with the telling. Through all the nearby villages people said that the lost heir to the King still lived and that he was as handsome as the sun.

Many princesses offered to be his bride. The King welcomed all the girls to his village, but he told them that he did not know what had happened to his lost son Then the princesses were married to the King's other sons.

One day the tall and graceful Princess Untombinde heard the story of the lost prince. At once she decided that this man must be her husband. She went to the village of the great King.

'Your King has an heir as handsome as the sun, an heir whom no one has seen,' she said. 'I have come to be his bride.'

The mother of the lost heir looked at Untombinde and wished that her son could marry this beautiful princess. The King said that his heir could not be found and that she should marry one of his other sons. But, to everyone's amazement, Untombinde refused. Nor would she leave the chief's kraal. 'I will stay here until he returns and then I will be his bride,' she vowed.

The mother of the lost heir was so touched by Untombinde's courage that she built a hut for the girl and told her to wait in it until her son returned. As night fell on the first day of her stay, Untombinde retired to sleep in her new hut. To her surprise the mother brought meat and sour milk and set it beside her.

'This is bridal food,' said Untombinde. 'Why do you leave it here at night?'

74

'For years I have set out food for my missing son,' replied the mother. 'Now I put out bridal food in the hope that he will return.'

Untombinde slept through the night and in the morning found the food untouched. The next night the mother again put food into the hut. In the morning Untombinde saw that the hut had been entered and some of the food had been eaten.

'Did you not see who came into the hut?' asked the mother.

'I saw nothing,' replied Untombinde.

On the third night, the mother again put food into the hut. In the blackest darkness, Untombinde woke. Someone was touching her arm and a man's voice asked who she was. 'I am Untombinde and I am waiting to marry the King's heir,' she replied.

'The heir was lost many years ago,' replied the voice. 'Why do you not marry someone else?'

Untombinde replied that only the heir to the King was fit to be her husband. She heard someone eating the food and then she was left alone. Yet when Untombinde felt the latch on the door, it had not been unfastened.

By now the mother was filled with excitement. She felt sure that it was her son who was eating the food, but Untombinde had still not seen her visitor and could not say who he was.

The next night food was left again and at the darkest hour, Untombinde heard a man's voice in the hut with her. The voice told her to make a fire and, in the glow from the flickering flames, Untombinde saw that it belonged to a snake with a man's face.

'I am the King's lost heir,' said the creature. 'Years ago I went to hide under the ground because I was afraid that my brothers would kill me. Now this is the only form I can take.'

Untombinde begged the snake to wait until dawn and speak to his mother, who still mourned his loss. The weird creature shook its head and said that it must leave before dawn. Untombinde pleaded with it and at last the snake agreed that she could fetch his mother. Untombinde hurried to find her. When they returned, a handsome man was waiting for them instead of a snake.

'Because of the bravery of Untombinde, I am restored to my strength and beauty,' said the man.

His mother wept with joy. She took him to stand before the King, who was overjoyed at seeing such a handsome son. The marriage between the heir and Untombinde was arranged at once. A great feast was held, with dancing and merrymaking. And in the course of time, the lost heir came to the throne with Untombinde as his Queen.

8

The Horns of Plenty

Once, long ago, there was a large village compound with many huts. Women went about their work and happy children played on the grassy veldt. However, there was one thin little boy who was not happy. The boy's mother had died a year before and he was hungry and unloved. No woman in the kraal wanted the trouble of feeding the boy. He was turned away from hut after hut and no one listened to him or comforted him when he wept. The boy's father was still alive, but he went out hunting each day. When he came home tired in the evening, he had no time for the boy. The unfortunate little fellow became thinner and weaker.

Try as he might, he could please no one. One day he collected some firewood, hoping to please one of the women and be given a meal, but the woman only complained that the bundle of wood was too small. She beat the boy and turned him unfed away from her hut. 'I will leave these cruel people and never return,' vowed the boy.

As darkness fell, he went to the cattle pen and took one of his father's bulls. He scrambled on to its back and rode the huge creature far away across the veldt. At dawn the bull and the boy lay down to rest. However they had not rested long when they saw a cloud of dust approaching.

'That is a herd of cattle led by a strong bull,' said the bull. 'He will challenge me to a fight. But do not worry, I shall win.'

The thin little boy watched with fear as a huge bull approached. He pawed the ground and snorted noisily through his huge nostrils. He tossed his great head with the sharp horns and challenged the boy's bull to fight.

A ferocious struggle took place. The two animals charged and locked horns and slashed and kicked at each other. At last the boy's bull triumphed and their enemy went away with his herd.

The boy and the bull went on across the endless veldt. As night was falling, another huge bull confronted them, pawing the ground and breathing heavily.

'Get down from my back,' said the boy's bull. 'I must fight this second bull, but now I am tired and I shall not win. However, don't be afraid. When I am dead, cut off my horns and carry them with you. Strike them whenever you are hungry or in need and you will be given whatever you want.'

The boy was terrified to think that his friend would be killed and he would be left alone, but he had little choice in the matter. He slid from the bull's back and watched while a second fight took place. The bulls struggled until finally his friend breathed his last and slid to the ground dead.

The little boy wept. Then, remembering what the bull had said, he cut off the horns and carried them with him on his journey. Come what may, the boy was determined never to return to his own kraal.

As night was falling, the boy came to a hut, where he asked for shelter. The owner welcomed him indoors.

'I will gladly give you shelter,' the man said, agreeably enough, 'but I can give you no food. There is famine in this land and I have only weeds to eat myself.'

The boy smiled. He touched one of the horns and asked for meat and drink. Immediately more food than they could possibly eat appeared before them. The man was amazed. Both of them ate well and then they settled down to sleep.

The man realised the value of the horns, and was determined to have them himself. During the night, he hid the magical horns in a corner of his hut and replaced them with some old horns from one of his own dead bulls.

In the morning, the boy thanked the man for the night's

shelter and went on his way. He walked for many hours and, when he felt hungry, he touched one of the horns and asked for food. No food was set before him. Then the boy realised that he had been tricked.

He walked wearily back to the hut where he had slept the night before. He listened outside the door and heard the man touching and striking the magic horns and ordering them to set food and drink before him. But the horns would obey only the little boy. Nothing was set before the thieving man, and he became more and more enraged.

When the boy entered the hut, the man was terrified, for he feared the boy's magical powers. The man fled and watched from a safe distance. He did not dare to return while the boy remained. So the boy touched the horns and asked for food. A fine meal was set before him. When he had eaten, he settled in the comfortable hut, where he slept well all night. In the morning he left carrying the precious horns.

All morning the boy walked under the bright sun. At noon, he sheltered in the shadow of a rock and ate food set before him by the horns. Again he walked on, and as night fell he came to another hut.

'Will you give me shelter for the night?' the boy asked the man in the hut.

The man looked at the dusty, dirty boy. 'Be on your way!' he said. 'I don't want ruffians like you staying in my hut.'

Wearily the boy walked on until he came to a river. He washed in the cool waters and again touched the magical horns. 'Bring me fine clothes and brass ornaments with which to adorn my arms and legs,' he said.

At once these things were given to him. The boy put them on and, dressed like the son of a chief, he approached another kraal. The chief hurried out to greet him. 'Welcome, great one,' smiled the headman, bowing and calling for a feast to be prepared.

The boy stayed in the kraal for several years. Whatever he needed was brought to him by the horns of plenty. As the boy was so obviously wealthy, he was treated with great respect by his new friends. The chief's beautiful daughter was given to him as a wife and for the rest of his life, the little orphan boy lived in happiness and plenty.

9
The Proud Princess

Long ago, the Zulu people were ruled by a great King who had conquered lands that stretched from horizon to horizon. His enemies trembled with fear whenever they heard the marching feet of his invincible warriors. One day, as the armies returned from yet another victory, a daughter was born to the King.

'Because this girl has been born on the day when my enemies have fallen like grass before the scythe,' said the King, 'she will be the most loved of my daughters. When she grows to womanhood and comes of age, the celebrations will be such as have never been seen before. Cattle will be driven in from the north and from the south, from the east and from the west. The dust from their hooves will rise in a huge cloud big enough to blot out the sun. The cattle will be slaughtered for a feast that will be greater than any feast ever prepared for a princess before.'

Victorious kings often spoke in such a way; the people expected it. Everyone knew that it was boastful talk meant to glorify the great victory of the soldiers, but everyone knew such boasts could not be fulfilled. Everyone knew these things except the little Princess.

The girl was beautiful and her proud mother often told her of the fine words spoken by her father, the King. The mother knew that the King meant that he would provide a very handsome feast for his beloved daughter, but the little girl believed all the words about the dust from the cattles' hooves rising up and blotting out the sun.

The Princess grew up with a very high opinion of her own importance and she became proud. However, as she was indeed the beloved daughter of the all-powerful King, no one corrected her and taught her more suitable behaviour.

At last the day came when the proud Princess was of age. As was the custom, she left the village and stood on the grassy veldt.

'Tell my father I am ready for him to drive the cattle before me, as he promised,' she said to her attendant girls.

The girls hurried away and the Princess waited for the cattle destined for her coming-of-age feast to be driven before her. The King ordered twenty oxen to be sent out. Twenty oxen was a very generous present for one girl. The proud Princess, who had believed every word about cattle coming from the north and from the south, from the east and from the west, could scarcely believe her eyes.

'Cattle? Cattle? What cattle?' she asked, looking around and letting her eyes pass over the twenty oxen as if they were not worth noticing. 'I see nothing!'

The herdsmen returned to the King and told him of his daughter's words.

'It is right that a great King should have a daughter who knows her worth,' said the King, through tight lips. He ordered the men to drive forty more oxen before his daughter.

Again the proud Princess was disappointed. 'I see nothing,' she sneered.

By this time the King was furious, but he did not wish to be shamed, so he ordered a hundred oxen to be driven out from the kraals.

Still the girl was not pleased. All her life she had expected to see thundering herds of cattle filling the veldt from horizon to horizon when she came of age, so she could not believe that these little groups of oxen were all she was to receive.

'Tell my father,' she said to the herdsmen, 'that the great, red sun is shining in the sky and until its light is hidden by the dust from the hooves of the cattle, I will not return home.'

The King was even more enraged by his daughter's words, but he would not be shamed by failing to provide his daughter with what she considered to be her due. He assembled his warriors and sent them to all the villages of his own tribe. From every kraal the King demanded a tribute of oxen. No one dared to refuse, so thousands of cattle were driven before the proud Princess.

She looked up. 'I can still see the great, red sun,' she said.

The King assembled an even greater army. He sent it out to

threaten the nearby tribes who, in fear, sent presents of cattle to stop the great King from destroying their homes. Still the Princess was not satisfied.

At last a band of warriors stumbled upon the entrance to a valley that none of them had seen before. To their surprise, they found grass greener and more luscious than in their own land and, best of all, the valley was filled with plump, healthy cattle.

'We will drive these oxen back to our King,' laughed the warriors. 'Even the proud Princess must be satisfied with the gift of so many fine beasts.'

The warriors crept to the narrow end of the valley and then, shouting and waving their arms, they drove the cattle out to the grassy veldt.

Suddenly they heard a voice calling to them from the mountainside. 'Why do you think you have the right to drive away my cattle?' asked the voice. Sitting among the bushes was a great hairy monster, the Lord of the Cattle himself, the magical spirit of the oxen. The cattle in the valley were his own perfect herd.

The Zulu warriors feared nothing and no one, so they shook their spears at the monster on the mountain. 'These spears give us the right to do exactly as we please,' they laughed. 'What have you to say to that, old furry feet?'

The Lord of the Cattle said nothing. He watched them go in silence.

The warriors drove the cattle across the plain and the dust from their hooves rose in a cloud that blotted out the sun. At last the proud Princess smiled and was satisfied. The King was delighted because now he would not be shamed. The cattle were slaughtered and a great feast was prepared.

The warriors did not tell the King about their meeting with the Lord of the Cattle. They did not want to displease him and spoil the celebrations.

After the feast, the proud Princess went to live in the hut of her mother and younger sister. For a few days, all was well. Then one day, as the sisters were resting in the hut out of the heat of the midday sun, the ground shook with violent thundering. The great furry monster, the Lord of the Cattle, was at the gate of the kraal. He broke down the fence and, as the girls rose to their feet to see what was causing such a commotion, two leaves blew into their hut.

'Go and fetch some water from the stream,' the leaves said to the younger girl. But to the proud Princess they said nothing.

The younger sister went to the stream and filled a jar with water but, when she turned to walk back, she found that she could not move her feet. they were rooted to the ground by magic.

The proud Princess was left all alone.

'Go to the next-door hut and fill a jar with water,' the leaves said to the proud Princess.

She laughed at them. 'Fetch water yourselves, if you want it,' she said.

The leaves repeated their order and something about them frightened the proud Princess into obeying.

When the Princess returned with the water, she was ordered to light a fire, then to grind corn and make bread. The proud Princess was furious; she had never done such lowly work in her life. 'My hands are not used to work,' she protested. 'Look! My nails are long. I cannot grind corn.'

The leaves trimmed the long fingernails of the proud Princess and set her to work. When the bread was baked, the leaves ordered the Princess to carry it with a calabash of milk to the gate, where the monster was waiting.

The Princess was too frightened to do anything but obey. As she walked through the village, the leaves followed her, stealing all the food they could carry from the huts. At the gate, everything was given to the monster, who swallowed it at once.

He looked at the Princess and said, 'Put on your finest clothes and wear your petticoat of beads. Put on your necklace of brass and your bracelets and your armlets.'

The trembling Princess did as she was commanded, then returned to stand before the monster.'Climb on my back,' he ordered. When she had done so, he turned and lumbered away.

All this while, the younger sister had been standing by the stream unable to move, but she knew in her heart what had happened. As the monster disappeared from sight, the sister's feet were freed. She ran screaming to her mother, who was working in the fields. The mother ran to her empty hut. She saw that the village had been robbed and told the other workers, who called the warriors. A band of soldiers gathered together and took up their weapons. They followed the trail of the great monster until they caught up with him.

'Give back the Princess,' the warriors shouted.

The Lord of the Cattle laughed at them. 'Do your feeble best to stop me,' he jeered. 'When you have done all you have to do, turn and go home.'

He stood still while the men threw their spears at him, but no weapon could pierce his thick hide. Still laughing, the monster turned and crashed away through the bush towards his secret valley. The bravest of the men followed him, but at last they realized they were wasting their time and, weak with weariness, they went home. The proud Princess was alone, riding on the back of the furry monster, the Lord of the Cattle.

On they went into the valley with the rich, green pasture, and then up the mountain slopes until they reached a bare, bleak cave. Inside were a pillow, a sleeping mat and bread and water.

'You will live here for a year and a day,' said the monster to the Princess. 'No one will cook your food. No one will clean for you. You will learn not to be proud. Your father humbled me by taking my cattle, now you must become humble in return.'

For a year and a day the proud Princess lived a harsh and uncomfortable life in the cave. At the end of that time, the monster allowed her to walk back to her own home. How pleased the girl was to return to the comforts of the village. After that, she was grateful for everything put before her and never again demanded enough cattle to blot out the sun.

10

Tricky Mr Rabbit

This and the story on page 68 – The Clever Monkey *– come from the west coast of Africa and are much more light-hearted than the Zulu stories. Anyone who reads many of these tales may see in them the roots of the Brer Rabbit stories told by the Blacks of the United States.*

Once, long ago, there was a cunning rabbit who enjoyed playing tricks on the other animals. The bigger the other animals were, the more Mr Rabbit enjoyed the joke.

One day Mr Rabbit was walking by the sea when he saw Mr Elephant.

'How big you are, Mr Elephant!' said Mr Rabbit. 'How big your feet are. Why I declare I have never seen such big feet on any other creature.'

The rabbit trotted round the elephant's feet pushing and prodding at them.

'Clumsy feet some people would call them,' laughed Mr Rabbit. 'How do you avoid tripping over with huge feet like that at the end of your legs? I feel sorry for you, Mr Elephant, having big, clumsy, awkward feet like that!'

Mr Elephant did not care to hear such talk. 'You are an impudent creature, Mr Rabbit,' he said. 'I feel like giving you a good spanking.'

The rabbit laughed and ran in circles round the elephant. 'I feel like tying a rope round your middle and dragging you into the sea. That's what I feel like doing,' jeered the rabbit.

This talk from a small rabbit made the elephant really angry. 'What, you! Tie a rope round a big fellow like me and drag me into the sea!' he trumpeted. 'You could not possibly do it. What nonsense!'

The rabbit took a coil of rope from his back. 'Let me tie this rope round you,' he said, 'and if I cannot drag you into the sea, then you have my permission to give me a good beating. I will stand still while you do it.'

'Agreed,' laughed the elephant, allowing the rabbit to tie the rope round his waist.

Then the rabbit ran to the seashore with the other end of the rope and spoke to a whale. 'Mrs Whale,' he said. 'You are big and I am little, but I bet that I can tie this rope round your middle and drag you up on to the land.'

The whale roared with laughter. 'Indeed you cannot,' she said. 'Why, what a big opinion you have of yourself, you little bundle of fur. But you can try if you wish. I have nothing else to do this fine afternoon.'

The whale kept still as the rabbit tied the rope round her middle.

'Now,' smiled the rabbit, 'you pull hard on this end of the rope and I will go and pull on the other.'

The whale started to swim out to sea, as the rabbit hurried back to the elephant.

'Mr Elephant,' called the rabbit, 'I am starting to pull you into the sea. Stop me if you can.'

The elephant felt the strong tug on the rope as the huge whale swam out to sea. He was amazed at the rabbit's strength and pulled with all his might to stay in the same place.

Meanwhile, in the sea, the whale was astonished to find herself being held back. 'How can that tiny rabbit stop a huge whale like me from swimming forward?' she gasped. 'How shameful to be out-pulled by a rabbit!'

Mrs Whale flapped her huge tail from side to side and heaved forward in the water. The elephant felt himself being dragged towards the beach. Step by step he was pulled to the very edge of the water and all the while the rabbit was hiding behind a bush and laughing fit to split his sides.

When his feet were splashing in the sea, the elephant saw that the other end of the rope was tied round a huge whale. 'Mrs Whale!' he called. 'Have you been speaking to a rabbit?'

Mrs Whale looked round and was amazed to see an elephant pulling at the other end of the rope. 'Indeed I have,' she said. 'Tell me, why are you pulling at the rope? The rabbit should be pulling.'

'We have both been tricked,' shouted Mr Elephant. 'Come near to the shore and let me untie this rope.'

While Mr Rabbit was having a great laugh, the elephant used his trunk to untie the rope from himself and Mrs Whale. Mr Rabbit, being no fool, ran away before the rope was completely undone.

At last Mr Elephant threw off the rope and looked round. 'I will catch that rabbit and give him a beating no matter how far ahead of me he is,' vowed the elephant.

He set off after the rabbit and soon he was gaining on him. The elephant was very cross as he ran with long strides on his big feet, following the rabbit.

Realising that soon he would be overtaken, the rabbit hid in the skull of a horse. The elephant came panting along and said, 'Mr Skull, have you seen a rabbit running this way?'

'Indeed I have,' the skull seemed to reply, but of course it was really the rabbit calling from inside the skull. 'Indeed I have,' said the skull, 'only then I was a horse. That rabbit spoke to me cheekily and I was about to give him a kick, when he stared at me with burning eyes and pointed a finger at me and in a second turned me into what you see before you.'

The elephant stopped and stared at the skull. He gulped and turned for home. 'Well,' he said, 'if that rabbit ever comes this way again, don't tell him that I was chasing him. Don't even tell him that you saw me. I have decided I don't want to catch him after all.'

As soon as the elephant was out of sight, the rabbit crawled out of the skull and ran off home, laughing all the way.

11

The Cunning Man

Malawi is an African republic that lies to the south of the Equator. It is a landlocked country bordering the enormous Lake Malawi, which is 344 miles (550 kilometres) long. Maize and corn are the main crops. The official language is English and old stories from this land were recorded by early English settlers.

Once, long ago, there was a great famine in the land and a certain cunning man decided to save himself from hardship. He went out into the forest and picked some wild figs. Then he walked on until he found a man who was so hungry that he was eating grass.

'Would you like to eat these figs?' asked the cunning man.

'Yes, indeed,' replied the other man, eagerly taking the fruit.

When all the figs were gone, the cunning man asked, 'What are you going to give me in return?'

The hungry man looked at him in surprise. 'I thought the figs were a gift because you felt sorry for me,' he said. 'I didn't know I had to give anything in return.'

'Come, come, what nonsense!' shouted the cunning man, standing up tall and glaring down. 'Of course you have to give me something. Why should I give a gift to a complete stranger? This was a trading arrangement. Don't try to escape your part of the bargain now, you cheat!'

The man who had been eating grass was so upset by all the shouting that he gave the cunning man a fishing net to silence him and make him go away.

The cunning man went on beside the lake. Soon he came to some men who were failing to catch fish with their hands.

'Why are you doing such a foolish thing as to try to catch fish with your hands?' asked the cunning man.

'Because we are so poor that we have had to sell our fishing nets,' they replied.

At once the cunning man held out the fishing net he had taken from the man who had been eating grass. 'Would you like to use this net?' he asked.

'Thank you,' said the men. They took the net eagerly and caught a good supply of fish from the lake.

No sooner was this done than the cunning man said, 'Half those fish are belong to me. They are payment for using my net.'

The fishermen were amazed. 'We thought you lent us the net because you felt sorry for us,' they said.

'How ridiculous! Business is business!' shouted the cunning man. 'What sort of thieves are you that you try to cheat me of my dues? Why should I, a stranger, give you something for nothing? You must have known from the beginning there would be a price to pay for using the net. Don't try to go back on your bargain!'

The fishermen were so upset at being accused of bad faith that they gave half the fish to the cunning man. He then walked on his way until he came to a village where the people had porridge to eat, but nothing to give it any flavour.

'Porridge on its own is dull food,' said the cunning man. 'Would you like some of my fish to cook?'

'How very kind,' smiled the people of the village, thinking that the stranger was willing to share his food with his fellow men in their time of trouble. No sooner had the fish gone down their throats, than the cunning man held out his hand.

'What are you giving me in return for my fish?' he asked.

'We didn't know we had to give anything,' said the village people in surprise.

'Don't try those tricks with me,' shouted the cunning man. 'A man gave me a fishing net in return for some figs. The fishermen gave me half their catch of fish in return for the use of the fishing net. Why should you not give me something for those fish you have eaten? Why should you get something for nothing?'

He made so much commotion that the village people gave the cunning man a supply of millet, with which he happily made off along the road. Further on, he came upon some men who were eating white ants.

'Ants are not food for decent people,' said the cunning man.

'We know that,' replied the men, 'but we have nothing else.'

'Would you like this millet?' asked the cunning man. The men at the roadside gladly accepted it and ate it. Immediately the cunning man asked for something in return.

'A man who was eating grass gave me a fishing net. Some fishermen gave me half their catch of fish in return for the use of the net. Some village people gave me millet in return for fish. What are you going to give me for the millet?' he shouted.

When they heard what other people had given to the cunning man, the men at the roadside dared not refuse him and they gave him some fine guineafowl feathers of great value. Feeling pleased, the cunning man continued on his way until he met some men who were dressing themselves up in the leaves of a maize plant. They saw the guinea feathers in his hand and asked for them.

'Those feathers will give a fine finish to our grand outfits,' they said. The cunning man agreed to hand the feathers over in return for a goat, that he drove on before him to the next village.

By this time night was falling and the cunning man asked for shelter for himself and his animal. The kind villagers allowed the cunning man to pen his goat in with theirs and to sleep in one of their huts. During the night, the ungrateful fellow got up and killed his goat. In the morning he made a great fuss, shouting and wailing at the loss of his fine animal.

'Your animals trampled it in the night!' he shrieked. 'You should have warned me that your goats were bullies. Now you owe me something in return.'

To rid themselves of such a troublemaker, the villagers gave him an ox, which pleased the cunning man. He drove the ox to his own home where he slew it and, taking the tail, he hurried to another lakeside village where he planted the tail in the mud. He set up a great wailing and shrieking until the men of the village came running to see what was the matter.

'My ox! My ox!' wailed the cunning man, pointing at the tail sticking up out of the mud. 'I was driving it along this path, when it slipped into the mud and sank. If it is you village people who made this path, then you are in great trouble. Fancy building a path through such a dangerous place! It is your fault that my ox is lost.'

When they heard those words, the men of the village grasped the ox's tail and heaved and pulled, doing their best, as they thought, to pull the unfortunate ox out of the mud. Of course the tail came away in their hands.

'Fools! Fools!' screamed the cunning man. 'Now you have pulled the tail from my ox, all hope of saving it is lost. Oh you wicked bunglers! What are you going to give me in return for an animal of such value?'

The simple village people were so upset at such dreadful accusations that they gave the cunning man twenty cattle in return for the one ox, which, in fact, had not been lost at all.

The cunning man drove the cattle home, feeling happy, as well he might. He had made a handsome profit from picking a few wild figs from the forest.